MAKING PLANNING WORK

a guide to approaches and skills

MAKING PLANNING WORK

a guide to approaches and skills

Cliff Hague
Patrick Wakely
Julie Crespin
Chris Jasko

ITDG
PUBLISHING

Intermediate Technology Publications Ltd
Schumacher Centre for Technology and Development
Bourton on Dunsmore, Rugby
Warwickshire CV23 9QZ, UK
www.itpubs.org.uk

First published in 2006

ISBN 1-85339-648-6
ISBN 978-1-85339-648-9

Intermediate Technology Publications Ltd. Is the wholly-owned publishing company of Intermediate Technology Development Group Ltd (working name Practical Action). Our mission is to build the skills and capacity of people in developing countries through the dissemination of information in all forms, enabling them to improve the quality of their lives and that of future generations.

Cover design and page layout by Graham Barker
Typeset by Thomas Brandi
in Amasis MT, Frutiger and Kipp
Printed in India.

TABLE OF CONTENTS

Foreword

Anna Kajumulo Tibaijuka
Under-Secretary-General and Executive Director
United Nations Human Settlements Programme (UN-HABITAT)

Planning has been for some time in a state of flux. Physical planning or Master Planning, as it was widely practiced a few decades ago has undergone several mutations including advocacy planning, participatory planning and budgeting, and community design. These mutations have been due, at least in part, to organic change within the profession. While no one person or group of people have taken the lead, planning has nonetheless been modernizing itself in a myriad of ways to respond to the challenge of and the quest for sustainable urbanization.

The seeds planted at the Habitat Agenda, adopted by the world's governments in Istanbul in 1996, are now coming to fruition with a wide range of initiatives that are revitalizing the practice of planning around the globe. Most of these initiatives share a common root in an ethical commitment to participatory governance and social inclusion, to reducing poverty and promoting environmental justice.

Making Planning Work looks at some of the key skills that underpin the new spirit of planning. These skills include effective means of communication between all stakeholders, mediation between competing or conflicting interests and, most importantly, collective reflection and learning. It also captures the essence of many innovations that have made planning work for bringing about change and lasting improvements to the living environment.

The World Urban Forum held in Barcelona in 2004 provided an important platform for exchanging experiences and ideas on the reinvigoration of planning on the global stage. As a follow up, the World Urban Forum to be held in Vancouver in 2006, has deliberately made space for taking this process further. There will not be unanimity on the future of planning, nor should there be. It is my sincere hope, however, that this publication and the continuing debate will further enrich the range of norms, tools, instruments and skills that are making new urban planning an increasingly relevant contribution to achieving more equitable, just and sustainable cities and communities worldwide.

Anna Kajumulo Tibaijuka

Preface

This guide was prepared for the United Nations World Urban Forum III and the World Planning Congress in Vancouver in June 2006. The aim of the guide is to focus international attention on the urgent need to increase global understanding of sustainable urban development processes and pro-poor planning practices.

Although the text refers extensively to 'planners', it is for all those engaged in the processes of planning and managing towns, cities and settlements: political leaders, professional planners, engineers, architects, lawyers, health and social professionals and technicians, and many others in national, regional and local government, non-governmental organizations, community-based organizations and private sector consultancies and enterprises, all of whom have a vital contribution to making and maintaining sustainable settlements.

Section 1 explains why a step-change is necessary. There is a need for more people with the knowledge and skills to make a difference but, equally important, new skills and attitudes are required, especially in conditions of rapid urbanization and the urbanization of poverty.

Section 2 demonstrates ways in which professionals and NGOs are creating and delivering innovative responses, often in situations of extremely scarce resources and conflictive competition for access to resources. Not all the examples are 'best practices'; successful innovators are those who learn from their mistakes. Nor is it suggested that all practices are transferable from one country or city to another. Transfer can only be based on local judgements and understanding of different cultures and values. We ask only that those who read this guide reflect on whether their own skills and practices could be enhanced, and whether the skills discussed here could help to make settlements more sustainable.

Section 3 briefly looks to the future. Its tone is optimistic, but not utopian. The global challenge of urbanization is daunting, but as Section 2 shows, imagination and skills can make an impact. This guide is a start, and hopefully a catalyst. It does not pretend to be comprehensive. Many readers will have experiences of their own of making planning work. We invite them to share those ideas.

The guide is an introduction to a website – www.communityplanning.net. The website invites everyone to respond and to add to the material in the guide. The site is regularly updated and can be a focus for the ongoing development of skills, ideas and easily accessible life-long learning. Hopefully, on the road from Vancouver in 2006 to the next World Urban Forum in Nanjing in 2008, this printed note will be overtaken by the website and by new learning networks and initiatives initiated by others. Developing and using skills for new approaches to urban development and planning, and learning from those experiences, must be a dynamic and inclusive process.

Abbreviations and Acronyms

BEN — Black Environment Network (UK)
CAP — community action plan
CBO — community-based organization
CCODE — Centre for Community Organization and Development (Malawi)
CDC — community development council
CIS — Commonwealth of Independent States
CLIFF — Community-Led Infrastructure Finance Facility
CODI — Community Organizations Development Institute (Thailand)
CSO — civil society organization
DCC — Dhaka City Corporation (Bangladesh)
DFID — Department for International Development (UK)
DSK — Dushtha Shasthya Kendra (Bangladesh)
DWASA — Dhaka Water Supply and Sewerage Authority (Bangladesh)
ESPON — European Spatial Planning Observation Network
GIS — geographical information systems
GPS — global positioning system
HIPC — highly indebted poor countries
HRD — human resource development
ICIWF — Information Centre of the Independent Women's Forum (Russia)
IDB — Inter-American Development Bank
IDP — Integrated Development Plan
IMF — International Monetary Fund
IWMI — International Water Management Institute (Ghana)
LASDAP — Local Authority Service Delivery Action Plans (Kenya)
MDG — Millennium Development Goal
MHPF — Malawi Homeless People's Federation
NDB — township development committee (South Africa)
NGDO — non-governmental development organization
NGO — non-governmental organization
NSDF — National Slum Dwellers Federation (India)
P3DM — participatory three-dimensional modelling
PAFID — Philippine Association for Intercultural Development
PRSP — poverty reduction strategy paper
RCIS — Rebuilding Community Infrastructure and Shelter (Sri Lanka)
RPP — Roma Participation Programme (Bulgaria)
RTPI — Royal Town Planning Institute (UK)
SDI — Shack Dwellers International
Sida — Swedish International Development Cooperation Agency
SPARC — Society for the Promotion of Area Resource Centres (India)
UCDO — Urban Community Development Office (Thailand)
UNDP — United Nations Development Programme

Acknowledgements

The guide was made possible by a grant from the UK Department for International Development and the Royal Town Planning Institute.

An advisory board provided support and direction throughout its preparation and we wish to acknowledge its members: Keith Thorpe, Head of the Urban Policy Support Team in the Office of the Deputy Prime Minister; Kelvin MacDonald, Director of Policy and Practice at the RTPI; Michael Parkes, United Nations and Commonwealth Department, DFID; Helen Walker, Academy for Sustainable Communities.

Above all, we wish to acknowledge the invaluable help of all those who provided material for the case studies, whose names and contacts are given in Section 2. Without their assistance and insights, the guide would be of little value.

In addition we wish to thank all the other people who generously provided advice and information, notably: Adriana Allen, Tom Carter, Julio Dávila, Judith Eversley, Jorge Fiori, Pascal Hofmann, Paul Jenkins, Eleni Kyrou, Caren Levy, Michael Mattingly, Michael Murray, Patrice North, Michael Safier, Jordi Sanchez, Harry Smith and Robin Thompson.

Cliff Hague
Patrick Wakely
Julie Crespin
Chris Jasko

Section 1

MAKING THE CASE

Section 1
MAKING THE CASE

For the first time ever, more people live in towns and cities than in rural areas. This opens enormous opportunities for the advancement of humankind. It also creates problems and misery. Timely and appropriate action, internationally and locally, can mitigate these problems. The guide is a small, but optimistic, contribution to this end.

This first section explains why urbanization is now a matter of global importance. Chapter 1 outlines the problems that already confront town and city managers, planners, developers and residents and that will dominate urban agendas for the next generation. The scale and immediacy of the issues are daunting. Chapter 2 points to ways forward, stepping stones towards more sustainable settlements.

1 Why an urbanizing world needs new approaches to settlement planning

1.1 Cities: The engines of national and regional development

The growth of human settlements is a crucial dynamic of the 21st century. The world's urban population will continue to grow. Built-up areas will expand on a scale never before known. The questions are how to improve the quality of life of this growing urban population, and how to steer the development of settlements towards a more sustainable path.

Globally towns and cities are growing by 65 million people a year. In 1950, 700 million people lived in urban areas (28 per cent of the world's population) and there were only 65 cities with a population of over a million. By 2000 the world's urban population was 2.8 billion (47 per cent of the total population) and there were 300 'million cities'. By 2015 there are likely to be 360 'million cities', with 150 of them in Asia.

City populations grow in two ways: first, because of the natural increase in their existing population – the live birth rate is higher than the death rate; and second, by the migration of people from the countryside and smaller towns in search of the opportunities that large towns and cities provide. Each day for the foreseeable future will see an additional 200,000 people living in towns and cities across the globe.

There are significant regional differences. In Europe and North and South America, the vast majority of people (around 75 per cent of them) are already urban dwellers. In the Americas urban growth continues, though in Europe it is almost static.

In Africa and Asia currently around 60 per cent of the people still live on in non-urban areas, but huge changes are happening. The urban population of African is growing by nearly 4.5 per cent per year and in Asia by 3.5 per cent.

The concentration of people in towns and cities brings great benefits and opportunities. Urban areas are the centres of trade, commerce and industry that underpin national and regional economic development. Nearly all manufacturing takes place in urban areas, where the size and diversity of urban labour markets allow businesses in both the formal and informal sectors to access and manage the workforce and markets that they need. National and regional income depends primarily on the buoyancy of the urban economy. Agriculture and other primary industries – mining, fishing, forestry – depend on urban areas to provide their markets and the range of goods and services upon which they rely – communications, technology, finance, banking, insurance – as well as linkages to the global economy.

Towns and cities are the centres of social development and cultural change that have impacts far beyond their boundaries. They are the hubs of national and regional service provision – education, health, security. They provide the centres of intellectual and technical advance, political development and artistic expression. Urban areas not only provide formal educational opportunity, they have always been places of social and cultural exchange and the generation of new ideas. Innovation – so crucial in the 21st century – at all levels is a product of sharing space and of building networks between people and institutions. The movements of people, goods and ideas, and the networks that connect cities and towns across the globe are the energy that sustains an economy and fosters life opportunities.

However, the way that urban growth is currently happening cannot ensure an acceptable quality of life, let alone an improvement in it, for the vast majority of urban citizens. The release of affordable and appropriately located land does not meet the needs for new housing and enterprises. The extension of urban infrastructure, services and amenities is not keeping pace with the growth of urban populations. Traffic congestion imposes ever increasing costs and damage to the environment that may be irreversible. The widening gap between rich and poor frays the social fabric. Vulnerability and risk, both short-term and long-term, are now acute.

These impediments to the effective and efficient functioning of towns and cities seriously constrain their capacity to act as the 'engines of national and regional development'. If large settlements cannot provide a well educated and healthy workforce, reliable infrastructure and accessible and effective services, then international and national companies will not locate and invest in them and local enterprises will not operate effectively or efficiently. If they cannot ensure a degree of social harmony and the freedom of cultural expression, then the resulting discord will erupt in class and ethnic divisions and conflict and will spill over to their hinterlands and beyond, further deterring investment in the creation of jobs, incomes and public revenue. Such is the circle in which planning, if it can be made to work, has a pivotal role.

A century ago the skills of town planners, architects, civil engineers, surveyors and public health professionals created workable solutions to the problems of urban growth and industrialization in the North. These were transferred to the developing countries of the South, but often with scant, if any, regard for the very different economic, demographic and social conditions. This has tended to result in the fossilization of 'planning' as a (largely) public sector activity, to the exclusion of planning as a process that engages a wide range of public, private and civil society actors. Even in the North the context in which planning now operates has changed significantly in response to the need to regenerate former industrial towns and to engage with communities through Local Agenda 21 and new forms of governance. A new and updated set of skills is now needed to make 21st century settlements sustainable in both the North and the South.

1.2 The urbanization of poverty and its implications

As ever more people live in urban areas, the geography of poverty also changes. In the last century, poverty was mainly equated with rural areas, especially in the poorer countries: development policies were targeted accordingly. Now, and for the future, most of the world's poor will be urban dwellers. This has two implications.

First, the achievement of international targets for poverty reduction – the Millennium Development Goals (MDGs) – more than ever depends on the management of urban areas. The economic performance of cities increasingly defines national economic performance. The juxtaposition of large-scale physical infrastructure and human capital that is the essence of an urban economy – both formal and informal – critically influences national well-being. Thus, urban development policies and effective urban planning can be a means of taking people out of poverty.

The second implication of the urbanization of poverty is the need for equitable urban development to deliver a reduction in poverty. Though overall urban economic growth is a necessary condition for poverty reduction, it is not a sufficient condition. Increasingly we are seeing a widening gap between the very rich and the very poor within the same cities. In many rich cities, suburbs and regions in the North, a developing 'hour glass' labour market is resulting in more 'good jobs' and 'poor jobs' with fewer opportunities in the middle. Wage inequalities are increasing almost everywhere in the developed world, even in countries that have strong egalitarian traditions such as Sweden.

Gross disparities in living conditions, poor housing, lack of access to essential services and jobs, social segregation and social exclusion sustain poverty, undermine security and erode the fabric that makes cities work economically – their capacity to concentrate large numbers of diverse people in an efficient manner. Unless there are positive planning strategies in place it is unlikely that poor communities, whether they be in the North or in the South, will be able to enjoy the benefits of urban economic success.

Poverty Reduction Strategy Papers (PRSPs), promoted by the World Bank, are now widely accepted national policy instruments for anti-poverty efforts. Many PRSPs are seriously flawed as they fail to recognize the basic differences between urban and rural poverty and the different strategic approaches that each requires. For instance, slums and informal settlements have become the definitive urban form under conditions of rapid urbanization and inappropriate land policies and management. Over 60 per cent of the urban population of Africa live in slums, and slums accommodate more than three quarters of the growth in Africa's total urban population. National and local governments throughout the developing world now struggle to find ways to legalize and upgrade illegal and under-serviced settlements. Yet adequate housing and security of tenure are vital to reducing poverty in urban areas.

1.3 Environmental imperatives

Concentrations of people and economic activity change environments dramatically. Another one billion urban residents over the next 15 years will significantly affect the global environment. Towns and cities and the process of urbanization have a significant impact on the local, regional and, ultimately, global environments. The vast majority of greenhouse gasses that deplete the ozone layer emanate from urban sources. The insatiable demand of cities for water, food and fuel has led to long-term changes in the natural landscapes of urban regions and beyond, all around the world. The demands of urban consumption of timber and its by-products account for much of the world's deforestation.

In the expansion of urban areas land is being converted from farms and forests to urban uses. How this process of development is managed determines just how much land and how many rural habitats of ecological importance are lost and the environmental significance of the changes in land use. The unprecedented levels of urbanization that will happen in the next generation make it more, not less, important that peri-urban development and the reuse of land within existing urban areas is undertaken in an informed, efficient and sensitive manner.

Just as PRSPs need to address the spatial dimension of poverty, so too do strategies for environmental sustainability. New approaches to the planning and management of development are an environmental imperative; they will not be enough by themselves, but they form an essential part of the equation.

The challenges that are presented by contemporary urbanization must become a cause for international concern or they will become insuperable. They demand approaches and skills that are new to many professionals and stakeholders. Using such skills, the planning and management of urban development can become more effective and more sustainable.

The UN estimates that global warming could create 150 million refugees by 2050. In 2001, 170 million people were affected by disasters of which 97 percent were climate-related.

2 Pointers to sustainable settlements

2.1 No sustainable development without sustainable urbanization

Since the UN Conference on Environment and Development in 1992, the need for more sustainable approaches to development has been widely recognized internationally. However, there is still surprisingly little awareness of the significance of urban development and planning processes. The conventional understanding of sustainable development follows the definition in the Brundtland Report: 'development that meets the needs of the present without compromising the ability of future generations to meet their needs' (World Commission on Environment and Development, 1987).

Too often those quoting Brundtland stop at this point. However, the report went on to identify two key concepts at the heart of the idea of sustainable development. The first was 'the concept of "needs", in particular the essential needs of the world's poor, to which overriding priority should be given'. The second was 'the idea of limitations imposed by the state of technology and social organisation on the environment's ability to meet present and future needs'.

There has been a tendency for the sustainability discussion to concentrate on environmental issues and diminish, or even dismiss, the importance of the social and political and the economic and financial sustainability of development initiatives. Largely as a result of inadequate consultation, not to mention limited active participation, many development programmes and projects fail because they are socially inappropriate or politically unacceptable, or because they do not contribute to the economic development of their intended beneficiaries, or because their cost in use is too high to be maintained. There has to be a 'balanced score card'.

To achieve more sustainable forms of development overriding priority should be given to the needs of the poor and curtailing the excesses of the rich. Involving people in the development process is essential in order to nurture their sense of engagement and 'ownership'. This holds true both in the North and in the South: unless we can get the urban basics right – adequate housing, jobs, security, access to learning, environmental conditions – then the urban-based economic engine is at risk.

In short, there can be no sustainable development without sustainable urbanization, and there can be no sustainable urbanization unless the needs of the poor are at the core of urban planning and management. The poor cannot be at the core of urban planning and management unless they are directly engaged in the planning and management processes.

2.2 Governance, decentralization and subsidiarity

Governments alone cannot address the scale and nature of urban challenges nor effectively exploit the potentials that are pent up in towns and cities: potentials that are suppressed by poverty and a lack of 'voice'. Urban development and planning must engage a wide range of actors – public, private and civil society – at different levels of decision making – national, regional and local. This requires a new understanding of subsidiarity, recognizing the most effective levels of authority. It also demands new approaches to participatory governance.

To be effective, decisions should be taken as near as possible to the citizens affected by the decisions. This is the concept of subsidiarity – getting the level of decision making right. However, there is a universal resistance to devolving authority: many see it as a loss of power and do not recognize the associated benefits of divesting responsibility. In many states the presumption has been that national government is the level where power is best concentrated. However, regional and local governments are important decision makers in matters of urban development, and many actions can only be effective if they are decided upon at a neighbourhood level.

There is a common misconception that devolution means that every decision should be taken at local level. Decisions taken at too low a level are as ineffective as those taken at too high a level. Some decisions need to be taken internationally. Ecological systems are not defined by national boundaries. Many infrastructure networks have to be organized on a regional or national scale to operate effectively. Rural–urban movement has to be tackled at city–region scale. Decisions concerning the extension and management of infrastructure and distribution networks can only effectively be taken at the municipal level. Those concerning the management of local services belong to the neighbourhood level, while those dealing with specific communities can only be effective if they engage households and individual residents.

Central to the promotion and nurturing of good governance practices is the need to 'empower' local governments, civil society organizations and communities to take decisions and to 'enable' them to implement them. The skills of leadership, conflict resolution, negotiation, and achieving effective coordination, collaboration or integration are central to participatory governance.

2.3 Adequate shelter for all

Even in rich countries the very poor rarely live in houses that can be deemed adequate. Access to secure and decent housing that is affordable is fundamental to making settlements that are economically and socially sustainable.

A few of the wealthiest countries and, albeit with ever increasing difficulty, even some of the not-so-wealthy communist states, have been able to ensure decent housing for nearly all their urban population by subsidizing the cost of construction, management and maintenance. However, the vast majority of governments do not have the resources or political will to emulate such policies. Thus, despite the rhetoric around 'housing rights', shelter is seen as a consumer good that is the responsibility of the household. However, because the demand for suitably located and serviced land and housing is so much greater than supply, most poor urban households cannot afford to join the formal housing market and are forced to gain shelter through the informal and usually illegal housing supply systems. These are typified by insecurity of tenure, inadequate access to urban infrastructure and services, unhealthy overcrowding, and dangerous and disaster-prone dwellings. But they are affordable.

Traditional spatial planning approaches in many countries have tended to ignore the large and growing informal land and housing delivery process and have presumed that government agencies would directly provide housing for the poor. Town plans have defined orderly layouts for such housing with little regard to the realities of the market or the social and economic needs of the urban poor.

More enlightened urban administrations in the developing countries of the South have recognized the limits of public resources – both technical and financial – and have embraced the basic principles of an 'enabling approach' to low-income housing. This sometimes entails the government provision of land with secure title and basic infrastructure on which householders construct the dwellings that they can afford – sites-and-services. The principal challenge in this process is the identification and servicing of suitably located land in sufficient quantity.

The counterpart to 'enabling' the production of new housing is improving the existing housing stock to ensure acceptable levels of security, safety and amenity. As with sites-and-services, public sector support to those living in existing slums depends upon ensuring security of title to land and property and sufficient access to affordable services that will encourage households to invest in improving their housing and local environment – slum upgrading.

All of this implies a new set of inter-professional understandings, attitudes and skills.

2.4 Economic opportunity and services

Today, connectivity and innovation are vital to economic development. Networks – whether of infrastructure or knowledge, formal or informal – trigger innovation and open opportunity. Formal networks need planning, sometimes at a continental scale. One of the barriers to African development is the paucity of international connections within the continent. Most socially acceptable informal sector economic networks tend to be at the local level and are not confined to informal transactions alone. An important characteristic of the competitativeness of many cities of the South is the close linkages between the formal and informal sectors.

The informal sector is that part of the economy that is unregistered and unregulated by government, though it often has its own sets of rules and means to enforce them. It is not isolated. It constitutes a significant part of the overall urban economy, particularly in poorer countries, though it is more prevalent in poor areas of rich cities than is often appreciated.

From these brief generalizations two important conclusions can be drawn for those seeking to make more sustainable settlements. First, the urban economy must be a central concern of urban planning. Too often municipalities get tied down trying to manage things that are better left to individuals and the private sector (for example, beer halls or bakeries) and fail to focus on the more strategic economic issues that individuals or firms cannot tackle (for example, land supply for small- and medium-sized enterprises, efficient infrastructure corridors, and so on).

Second, the informal sector matters and urban planning needs to cater for it without destroying it. Attempts to legalize and regulate informal enterprises have almost invariably failed because doing so, by definition, removes their comparative advantage in the market. However, with the right understanding and skills, it is possible to sustain and create local economic activity in ways that do not destroy their markets but help to link them with the formal sector and mainstream urban economy.

To make settlements more sustainable planners and other officials need to understand business development and be aware of the livelihood strategies of the poor. People and communities in poverty in all parts of the world have complex and fragile survival strategies that can be upset by all but the most sensitive of interventions.

Institutions of governance need to strengthen and sustain the endeavours of the urban poor, not undermine such endeavours. Tapping the potential of local social networks and informal institutions is an important skill for those who work in formal government agencies or for private companies involved in the delivery of urban services.

2.5 Environmental justice and environmentally sustainable cities

If sustainable communities are to be fair and environmentally sensitive, there has to be fairness in the way that environmental impacts on settlements are assessed and remedial strategies are shared. Environmental inequity can exacerbate poverty. A gap exists in living environments not just between rich and poor countries but also between affluent neighbourhoods and poor areas within all cities. Poor households often lack access to safe water, so typically women spend time fetching water and thus have their opportunities for learning and employment limited, so the household remains poor. The car-owning upper-income groups can have a greater negative impact on the environment than charcoal-burning or water-polluting slum dwellers. Again, if sustainable development requires that overriding priority is given to the needs of the poor, then environmental policies and actions should not discriminate against the poor, indeed they must be pro-poor. Policy makers need skills to make the connections and to search for creative solutions that make environmental gains a step towards poverty alleviation.

2.6 Diversity and equity

Cities throughout the world are cosmopolitan. They are characterized socially by the diversity of the ethnic origins of their population. Although it is convenient to talk about 'the poor' to highlight the significance of poverty in discussion of sustainable development, the poor are diverse, and there can be significant differences and conflicts of interest among and between them. A clear understanding is needed of the different gender needs and abilities of women and men, age needs and capacities of the young and old, and cultural needs and expressions of different ethnic groups. The recognition of the cosmopolitan nature of cities and in particular their low-income neighbourhoods, many of which house urban newcomers from different regions and religions, is central to the success of any socially sustainable development.

Diversity presents a challenge: 'one size does not fit all'. The recognition of diversity is an essential first step to achieving inclusion and highlights the need for creativity and particular skills in the delivery of equal opportunities.

2.7 New times, new skills, new professionals

There are different traditions, even 'cultures', of planning in different countries. Planning has primarily been a state activity and so has been stamped by formal political systems and institutions. While traditional differences are likely to persist, it is clear that in many countries the legislation, institutions and skills involved in 'town planning' were nurtured from European 19th century ideas and formalized in the 20th century, but fail to match 21st century realities and needs. Rapid urbanization, the new significance of urban poverty and the need for more sustainable development make some modernization necessary in all planning traditions, though the form that the modernization takes will still reflect different cultures and priorities.

The nature of planning as a profession has also differed between countries. This is reflected in differing nomenclatures ('physical planners', 'town planners', 'urbanists' and so on) and professional entry requirements, often as part of national systems of registration. In the 20th century, the professional division of labour mimicked the production lines in the factories – discrete tasks undertaken by separate groups of people. It was an exclusionary tool to protect a privileged labour market position. Today's urban condition, especially in poor countries, has rendered this model obsolete. Professional boundaries need to be permeable (between profession and between professionals and non-professionals), with ladders of opportunity replacing the closed shop. Planning to make settlements more sustainable is a pluralist activity; many of the skills are generic and not unique to 'town planners' or any other professional category from the last millennium.

If we look beyond the confines of traditional professional boundaries and state institutions, beyond attempts to micro-manage land use and the discredited top-down, technocratic master plans from a previous age, then we can discern new approaches to planning and managing urban development. These put sustainable development and poverty reduction at the core. They recognize the multiplicity of actors and the limits of state power, engage with the private sector and civil society. We call these approaches 'planning' not because they are uniquely the work of professional planners, but because the integrative vision of the founders of 'town planning', encapsulated by Patrick Geddes as 'Folk, Work, Place', best expresses today's imperatives.

So it is 'planning', but maybe not planning as some have previously known it! While aspects of the old, technical know-how of professions are still important, established routines and relationships need to be overhauled. Skills such as creativity, a capacity to challenge assumptions and grasp the big picture, and governance skills such as communication and negotiation may not be entirely new. What is different is that today they are essential.

It is no coincidence that these are mainly 'soft', people-focused skills. To a considerable degree, we already possess the technical know-how to upgrade slums, create affordable, energy-efficient houses, provide safe drinking water, clear waste, connect neighbourhoods or create new settlements and build more sustainable communities. The barriers to overcome are erected by limited resources, bureaucracy and the lack of political will.

PRACTICES, PROCESSES AND SKILLS

Section 2

PRACTICES, PROCESSES AND SKILLS

Section 1 has demonstrated the global scale and significance of the urban challenge. As these challenges have been grasped, so themes such as poverty reduction, sustainable development and good governance have become central concerns of, and a common ground between, campaigning NGOs, civil society organizations and multilateral agencies. That is why, across the world, new understandings, approaches and skills are being developed and addopted. Subsidiarity and decentralization, for example, are integral to good government, but require inter-personal skills and a capacity to network across different scales and institutions, abilities that technocrats insulated behind closed doors in central ministries thought that they did not need in the past. Such skills can be learned, and will be required increasingly in the future.

Planning and management skills for the 21st century involve new ways of seeing, thinking, learning and acting. They are often referred to as 'generic' skills, because they can be shared, transferred between, and learned from, all those with a stake in the sustainable development of settlements – planners, politicians, academics, community leaders and citizens.

Section 2 shows that the application of these approaches is not only something that needs to happen or can happen, but is something that is happening in many different contexts around the world. Progress in planning through the use of new skills is occurring at all levels and in all sectors. As the examples and case studies in the following chapters show, this is having positive impacts on the sustainability, governance and level of social justice being achieved in development.

The chapters in Section 2 highlight skills rather than explain techniques. In other words, the aim is to explore approaches, attitudes and understandings that can underpin a new type of planning and management practice, but not to set out a prescriptive step-by-step approach saying 'this is what you need to do'.

The logic behind doing it this way is partly based on principle and partly on expediency. The principle is that international transfer fails when it is detailed and prescriptive; but can be a positive force when it is suggestive and indicative, a mirror held up to enable critical reflection on what is happening in one's own city. Therefore the aim is to share experiences, raise aspirations, and encourage and not to attempt to define standardized templates that cannot take account of different cultures and economies. The expediency is that this guide makes no pretence to be complete or rigorous in evaluating different experiences and practices. It is impressionistic with the intention of stimulating fuller and richer exchanges of experience.

Chapter 3 looks at cognitive and analytical skills – getting the understanding and information around which visions, plans and actions can be developed. Chapter 4 then emphasizes communication, negotiation and inclusion, the skills that are central to making planning pro-poor. Skills for strategic action are highlighted in Chapter 5 because strategy and vision are essential to change the unsustainable trajectory that many settlements are currently on. Management skills, the focus of Chapter 6, are central to planning and the effective use of scarce resources. Then Chapter 7 covers skills in relation to monitoring and learning, which are vital to enhancing capacity for making settlements more sustainable.

The chapters, each with a particular focus, are a way of putting the different examples and experiences in some order to help readers follow the text. However, in real life, practices do not come along neatly packaged; rather stages overlap, actions are fused together, and planning looks more like a complicated set of loops than a simple straight line. Therefore, the sequence of the chapters in this section is less important than the common themes that underpin the skills that are reviewed. Grasping what those commonalities are is important, but also subjective. To start that discussion, Caren Levy* suggests that key common themes are:

*Levy, C. (2005) unpublished notes, DPU, London, with references to Liedtka, J. M. (1998) 'Strategic thinking: Can it be taught?', in Long Range Planning, 3 (1), pp120–129.

- ☐ **being intent-focused**, allowing individuals within an organization to marshal and leverage their energy, to focus attention, to resist distraction and to concentrate for as long as it takes to achieve a goal;

- ☐ **diagnosing key relationships**, enabling planners to recognize where opportunities and constraints lie and how these relate to structures of power;

- ☐ **organizational strengthening**, including building capacity and strengthening alliances that can help convince those holding political power to surrender some of their stake and take a chance on alternative sources of knowledge;

- ☐ **leadership**, but to be effective it depends on dialogue and advocacy, which require listening, eliciting answers that express deeper interests, getting information from diverse sources, identifying interests and negotiating positions;

- ☐ **'thinking in time'** and **'thinking in space'**, or considering when and where actions can be taken and under what restraints in order to reinforce strategic action;

- ☐ **adopting a learning perspective** that expands the capacities of individuals and organizations involved in the planning process. Actors must not be both learners and knowers. For planners, this means continuous testing, monitoring, learning and sharing of lessons learned;

- ☐ **innovation and creativity**, not as luxuries but as essentials. Difficult situations cannot be turned around by old routines. Taking risks and having confidence in people is less dangerous than assuming that there is no need or scope to change the ways that things have always been done;

- ☐ **good management of projects**, people, finance, time and property as a fundamental platform for effective delivery of professional services. These skills are important every day and throughout a career. They are not just a matter for senior staff or administrators;

- ☐ **precedent setting** as the core of all the above ideas and innovations, demonstrating the effectiveness of new ways of doing things.

3 Analytical and Cognitive Skills

Urban change is rapid and increasingly discontinuous in nature, outpacing attempts to comprehend or catalogue it by using traditional approaches. Much planning thought and associated skills were forged in an era when it was assumed that professionals employed by governments could draw out the ideal arrangements of land uses to secure 'orderly development' that would then be undertaken primarily by other government agencies. There are few parts of the world where this mental model is still viable, and in many of the poorest countries it is now a dangerously unrealistic basis for action.

The dynamics of urban development are extremely complex; the drivers and their combinations will be unique to each particular place. There will never be enough resources to collect all the information, and even when information has been gathered it may be open to conflicting interpretations. 'Comprehensive' surveys were a rationalist fetish; they were always doomed to gather dust once the funds ran out or new change made them outdated.

The challenge is to hang on to the insight that 'everything affects everything else' – that urban development is an interplay of economic, social, environmental and cultural factors, not 'just' a matter of manipulating physical artefacts – while avoiding the paralysis of superficial understanding and insufficient information. This chapter explores ways to grapple with this challenge.

Analytical and cognitive skills are important, but they are insufficient on their own. They must be complemented by collaboration and communication, clear strategies, and good leadership and managerial skills (all of which will be looked at in subsequent chapters)

3.1 Understanding the environmental dimension of sustainable settlements

Urbanization in its present forms constitutes a significant threat to environments and ecological systems both locally and globally. While the rate of increase of urban populations is greatest in the South, the environmental damage done is mainly in the North. 15 per cent of the world's population living in high-income countries account for 56 per cent of the world's total consumption, whilst the poorest 40 per cent account for just 11 per cent of consumption. Skills to improve understanding of the environmental aspects of land use and development are therefore needed both in rich countries and in poorer countries.

Environmental protection is widely recognized as an important aim of land use planning systems in many countries, but traditional technical skills and tools, such as land use surveys tend to be static, even mechanistic. They have little resonance with those whose actions will ultimately determine the use of land, such as developers or politicians. So the issues are not just about information per se, but about how the information is shared with and understood by other stakeholders, how it gains credibility and acceptance as a means to build a consensus for action that will promote sustainable development.

What skills of information gathering and analysis are being used that might help to make planning work as a force for environmental sustainability? The first case study from the Philippines shows how 21st century technologies such as global positioning systems and geographical information systems (GIS) can be used in a participatory manner to improve natural resource planning and resolve conflicts over land.

Case Study 1: PHILIPPINES

Use of GPS and participatory 3D models to reclaim land on Mindanao

© G.Rambaldi/ARCBC 2002

On the island of Mindanao in the Philippines, Talaandig people are part of a new movement of indigenous community surveyors. Equipped with global positioning system (GPS) receivers, these surveyors have an ambitious goal – to delineate and reclaim their ancestral territories. Their GPS records are used to create accurate three-dimensional maps through an innovative process known as participatory 3D modelling (P3DM). Coordinated by the Philippine Association for Intercultural Development (PAFID) and sponsored by the European Union, P3DM initiatives are facilitating cooperation and effective decision making among indigenous communities and government planners in two important fields: land conflict resolution and natural resource planning.

In just over five years, PAFID and its community partners have mapped over a million hectares of ancestral domains. Due to their technical accuracy and detail, P3DM maps are now accepted by the government as proof of claims for legal recognition of ancestral land rights. Previously, the bulk of indigenous lands had not been properly surveyed and had been classified as state owned. Planning officials had designated large areas for mining, logging and military installations, which led to evictions, violent confrontations and the mass dispossession of many local communities.

The P3DM models are also proving invaluable in natural resource planning. Increasing pressure on diminishing resources, such as freshwater, forests and fish, make sustainable development plans crucial to the survival of small tribes. Because the physical three-dimensional features of a P3DM model are immediately recognizable, all members – including elders and those who cannot read – are able to participate in resource planning. Such models have been used in resolving inter-tribal conflicts over resources, most notably water, and in pointing out problem areas and solutions to government planners.

PAFID's experiences demonstrate that an intelligent combination of participatory decision making and modern technology can provide solutions to land conflicts and assist in natural resource planning. The secret of the success of the P3DM approach lies in its ability to engage both indigenous community members and the authorities in an ongoing political dialogue that is mutually beneficial.

Source:
Kevin Painting

Contacts:
Kevin Painting
Technical Centre for
Agricultural and Rural
Cooperation (CTA)
Postbus 380
6700 AJ Wageningen
The Netherlands
Tel: +31 (0) 317 467100
Fax: +31 (0) 317 460067
e-mail: painting@cta.int

Giacomo Rambaldi
e-mail: Rambaldi@cta.int or
grambaldi@iapad.org
Website: www.cta.int,
www.iapad.org,
www.ppgis.net

Case Study 1 demonstrates that sophisticated modern information technologies can help planners and other decision makers to better understand the need for a sustainable approach to resource planning. The case shows that GIS must be sufficiently flexible to include diverse and unexpected forms of community information (such as narratives, citizen reports, photographs) and to model scenarios that may diverge from local government priorities in a planning process. Successful implementation and sustainability of GIS analysis by non-governmental and community-based organizations needs both GIS provision and a support institution.

The example also shows that the today's technologies are effective when they build bridges in understanding. The crucial point in the case study is that the information is not solely the preserve of technologists, but is accessible even to persons who, though they cannot read, are important stakeholders in the area. Information is power, but that power is shared, and through that process there can be a resolution of long-standing conflicts. The techniques involved in operating global positioning receivers are important, of course, but the skill is about using the technique and the information to include, not exclude, other stakeholders.

The collective collection and sharing of information enhances understanding of how land can be developed in more sustainable ways and does not necessarily require the support of sophisticated technologies. Case Study 2 looks at a form of development and land use planning that it widely thought to work against sustainability – low density North American suburban subdivision. The case study shows how a shared understanding of the natural environment – and the property market – can change routines and create more sustainable outcomes.

Case Study 2: USA

How to make low density suburbia more sustainable, attractive and profitable

Randall Arendt is a powerful advocate of landscape conservation planning. His skills are sought by councils and by developers across North America because his designs are 'twice green' – delivering environmental quality in developments that sell well.

The secret of his success has been his ability to challenge creatively the mechanical land subdivision process that has rolled out hectare upon hectare of American suburbia. Normally homes and garages sit on standardized plots regardless of the nuances of the landscape and its ecology. Arendt has been able to persuade planners and developers to depart from the uniformity of 'cookie-cutter' layouts and to use the land that is 'saved' to protect trees, views, vernal pools, or the myriad other features that bring visual rewards and protect wildlife. As the population ages, those people with large plots, worn out by years of mowing lawns the size of football pitches, provide a growing market for the trade-off between private and public green space.

Contact:
Randall Arendt
e-mail: rgarendt@cox.net

For numerous free downloadable publications, see
www.greenerprospects.com

The quality of the conserved green areas adds a premium to the property price, and more imaginative lay-outs also save on costs for streets and utilities (and help to recycle water). "The predominant design standards operating in much suburban planning – on both sides of the Atlantic – are engineering standards covering grey infrastructure", says Arendt. 'We need to incorporate green infrastructure into by-laws and regulations as well, and to require that the principles of good site analysis be applied'.

He advocates a step-by-step approach to designing neighbourhoods: "I believe that one should begin by determining the open space first. If this is done, and if the regulations also require that a significant proportion of the unconstrained acreage be designated as conservation land, it is nearly impossible to produce inferior or conventional plans. The second step, after locating the preservation areas, is to select house locations, with homes positioned to take maximum advantage of the protected land that forms the neighbourhood squares, commons, greens, playing fields, greenways, farmland, or forest preserves. The third step involves 'connecting the dots' by aligning the streets and trails to serve the new homes".

He is passionate about site detail and the need to walk sites before judging designs: 'It is impossible to completely understand properties only by examining two-dimensional paper documents inside meeting rooms'. He takes members of planning boards (the US equivalent to planning committees) out on site, helping them determine those features that are most worthy of 'designing around'.

Arendt's work shows how something as basic as walking round a site and studying its features in detail can make a difference, and can be a way to share information and understanding with others involved in the planning and development processes. The context and the techniques in these two case studies could hardly be more different, but they show that the core skills are remarkably similar. They entail accurate and up-to-date collection and recording of relevant environmental information but in a way that is collaborative and comprehensible to non-professionals and other stakeholders. Similarly, though the issues of environment are central to both case studies, the understanding is not only environmental, but encompasses understanding of institutions and their cultures, whether these be tribal systems in the Philippines or planning boards and property markets in Pennsylvania.

3.2 Understanding the economic dimensions of sustainable settlements

Some countries have had a tradition of regional planning and regional policy, but this has often sought to subsidize regions whose economy is performing poorly. In general though, planning is thought of as a purely local matter. However, there have been significant changes in our understanding of the spatial aspects of competitiveness and economic growth in the last decade or so as knowledge and innovation have become increasingly important economic drivers. Access to networks matters more than geographical proximity; nodes and gateways have special advantages; transport links can create development corridors – or have a 'tunnel effect' by dumping noise and pollution on people who have no access to the network itself. These changes in the way that we understand space economies have resulted in a rethinking of information, skills, practices and even scales of planning and regional policy.

Case Study 3 looks at the development of cross-border and transnational planning in Europe and the skills being developed in collecting and analyzing information across and between spatial scales.

Case Study 3: EUROPE

Spatial planning and territorial cohesion

As the European Union has grown, so that it now encompasses 25 countries, so it has also embraced the need for sustainable development, international competitiveness and cohesion within the European territory. In 1999, the spatial planning ministers of the then 15 member states agreed the European Spatial Development Perspective. This is not a binding document – the EU as an institution has no legal competence in spatial planning. Rather it set out policy options that it urged member states and regional and local governments to apply. One of the foremost of these was the idea of polycentric urban development. This implies strengthening functional linkages and cooperation between urban centres with complementary strengths so that they can become more competitive and in this way the benefits of economic growth can be more widely shared around the European territory rather than being over-concentrated in the most developed area known as the 'Pentagon' (because it is bounded by London, Paris, Milan, Munich and Hamburg). One aim is to grow some of these polycentric urban networks into 'global economic integration zones'. Gateway cities – transcontinental entry points to the enlarging Europe – were also identified as having special economic potential.

New knowledge and skills are needed to take these ideas forward. The European Spatial Planning Observation Network (ESPON) began its work in 2002. It is mapping key spatial trends (for example, migration, accessibility, access to telecommunications), indicators and territorial impacts of policies across the 25 EU countries, plus Switzerland, Norway and the two countries that are candidates for EU membership, Bulgaria and Romania. The work is done in international teams and the analysis is conducted at three levels – macro (the 29 countries as a whole), meso (international groupings of regions in particular parts of Europe, such as the Baltic Sea Region) and micro (national and regional within a country). Attention is also being paid to neighbouring countries such as those in North Africa, and to 'Europe in the world'. Another project is exploring the spatial implications of competitiveness within a knowledge economy. The result is that the territorial aspects of development potentials can now be better understood, and policy dilemmas between different scales have been highlighted. For example, a policy that will close the development gap between the new member states from Eastern Europe and the older members from Western Europe will probably result in widening disparities between the capital cities of those new members and their rural or former heavy industrial regions.

Contact:
ESPON Co-ordination Unit
Technoport Schlassgoart,
66 rue de Luxembourg,
L-4221 Esch-sur Alzette,
Luxembourg
Tel: +352 54 55 80 700
e-mail: info@espon.lu

All ESPON reports can be
downloaded from
www.espon.lu

Thus ESPON is developing skills in the analysis of territorial potentials and in assessment of the territorial impacts of policies in fields such as transport, agriculture and research and development. It is using some innovative mapping approaches and developing a range of indicators that policy makers can use, as well as applying scenario-writing techniques to deepen awareness across Europe of the future implications of today's decisions and actions.

As with the other case studies, the techniques and results are only part of the story. In only four years ESPON has fostered dynamic knowledge networks across a whole continent. The incentive of being involved in an innovative research programme that is linked to practice has stimulated cooperation among teams drawn from many different countries, including new member states. The result is a sharing of knowledge and a building of capacity.

In the United States, the organization Social Compact is gaining understanding of informal economies. It is working to improve awareness of the scope for (re-)investment in low-income areas with large, highly productive informal economies. Social Compact's model is exposing innovative ways of looking at production and increasing prospects for improvements to neighbourhoods that have suffered from serious under-investment. The results, and once again the processes of getting and using the information, are bringing communities, the private sector and government into closer contact. This builds the potential for partnerships and for long-term benefits to a greater number of urban dwellers.

Case Study 4: USA

Measuring the informal economy at the neighbourhood level

In over 100 low-income neighbourhoods in the US, the non-profit organization Social Compact has conducted market analyses using its DrillDown technique. DrillDowns build business-oriented profiles using data from over 30 different sources to identify untapped market opportunities often overlooked by more traditional market analysis models. This new neighbourhood data is then disseminated to corporate, government and community leaders with the aim of spurring new investment and improving the lives of low-income residents. Social Compact has consistently found low-income communities to be much larger, safer and with greater buying power than previously acknowledged.

Social Compact's reports, which are available to all on-line, have helped to stimulate significant (re-)investment in low-income areas. In Houston, where Social Compact identified an informal economy worth over US$440 million in the neighbourhoods profiled, findings spurred the redevelopment of the Gulfgate Center, the first new construction in inner-city Houston for 50 years. Today, the Center enjoys 100 per cent occupancy and has created 2,000 jobs. A 246-unit condominium has also been redeveloped in the area. In Harlem, New York City, an informal economy of over US$1 billion was found. Following the publication of Social Compact's report, Fleet Bank (now Bank of America) established two new branches and three ATMs in the neighbourhood, as well as an aggressive and successful small business-lending programme for local residents.

Social Compact uses indicators common to local informal economies to capture the size and value of the production of unregulated (under-the-table payments made to day labourers, for example) and regulated goods and services that may be informally or illegally distributed (clothing, food and electrical goods). Indicators in this model include the ratio of the amount of money spent compared to the amount of declared earnings, the percentage of low-income households, the percentage of foreign-born people in an area, the number of households without a credit history, the method of bill payments and the prevalence of alternative financial institutions.

Social Compact uses a number of skills to ensure the greatest degree of success in each informal economy analysis. These include partnership building, communication, vision and organizational learning. Together, these skills strengthen Social Compact's key steps of building support and collecting accurate data, which serve later to give greater meaning and legitimacy to findings as they are put to use.

Social Compact works in close partnership with the private sector to respond to its demand for better market data on inner-city neighbourhood income. One driver for this demand is a suspicion that the large informal economies in low-income communities are not being captured by traditional market analyses. By listening to the corporate sector and directly addressing their needs, business leaders have become stakeholders in DrillDowns and have been critical to the framework and design of the model. Through partnerships and continual reappraisal, Social Compact has devised a dynamic and flexible model that captures key characteristics of informal economic activity in multiple markets that is formulated by, and with buy-in from, decision makers in the business sector.

In collecting data, Social Compact's informal economy model requires a broad range of inputs and therefore, a number of partnerships. In a typical case, Social Compact will need data from city departments, financial institutions and other private data sources. Social Compact has found that forging partnerships with government economic development agencies at the nascent stages of a project is the best way of engaging with other data providers. There are clear practical benefits to working with the city authorities. Depending on the project/analysis, the public sector may contribute much of the raw data needed. In addition, it may already have long and established relationships with the private sector. Finally, if technical capacity is limited, partnering with universities and other research organizations can offer technical support and academic expertise through GIS and existing research programmes.

The strength of the relationships forged in previous stages is often the deciding factor in the ultimate success of the neighbourhood market profile. From its outset, Social Compact has placed great emphasis on building buy-in and support from a broad coalition of decision makers from the public, private and non-profit sectors. This ensures that the informal market study is seen by all parties as a trusted and reliable information tool, which they helped to develop. Many cities, retailers, property developers and community groups have attributed the growing reputation of their neighbourhoods as areas ripe for investment to the DrillDown.

Source:
Jamie Alderslade

Contact:
Jamie Alderslade
Senior Research Analyst
Social Compact, Inc.
738 7th Street, SE
Washington, DC 20003
United States
Tel: +1 202 547 2586
Fax: +1 202 547 2560
Website: Www.social-compact.org

Social compact shows how market analysis skills can help people in poor neighbourhoods. Informal economies are significant for the livelihoods of the poor in both rich and low-income countries, yet in the past they have been largely ignored in the data collection undertaken by planners. The DrillDown technique may or may not be appropriate in situations outside the US, but the underpinning skills of networking to spot hidden potential most certainly are approaches that can be transferred.

3.3 Understanding the social dimensions

Diversity is difficult for many officials who are used to serving the public interest by treating everyone the same. It is very easy to assume that lifestyles and values that are familiar among officials themselves are common to everybody else. Yet livelihoods differ between individuals and along lines of gender, age, socio-economic status, ethnicity, religion, ability and culture. Skills are needed to understand the differences and the conflicts of interests at play in any urban context (see Chapter 5).

Needs and priorities encompass not only material items and income. Livelihood also implies relationships, experiences and ideas that are all linked to the environment in which people live. Planners and professionals with tertiary education and the social status that goes with it, can rarely tackle poverty in an effective and sustainable manner without understanding the way ordinary poor people experience and survive the city.

Stakeholder analyses should underpin how information is accumulated throughout any planning process. Such a perspective will alert decision makers to how other parties view development, and is essential when preparing for negotiation and external communication (see Chapter 4). Exposing information to different users and interpretations can also empower excluded groups and change assumptions that have gone unquestioned in the past. Difference can be a powerful stimulus for creative thinking.

Established data sources can easily hide the poor through crude simplifications such as the use of statistical averages, or simply because the conditions and aspirations of the poor are difficult to record accurately. Case Study 5, the self-enumeration of pavement dwellers in Mumbai, shows how deep-rooted barriers can be overcome and information can become a force for progress. Pavement dwellers made themselves visible to government officials and the rest of the city and raised awareness of their conditions. By creating and disseminating information on their community, their lives and the problems they face, they managed to change stakes in their favour, impacting on urban policy and perceptions among city officials.

Further information:
Burra, S. (2000) A Journey Towards Citizenship: The Byculla Area Resource Centre, Mumbai, Development Planning Unit Working Paper No. 109 (May), Development Planning Unit, University College London
Mohapatra, B. N. (n.d.) Civil Society and Governance: From the Vantage Point of the Pavement Dwellers of Mumbai, unpublished report
Patel, S. and Mitlin, D. (2001) The Work of SPARC, the National Slum Dwellers Federation and Mahila Milan, India, IIED Working Paper series on Poverty Reduction No. 5 (December), IIED, London
SPARC (1985) We, the Invisible, SPARC, Mumbai, India
SPARC website: http://www.sparcindia.org

Sources:
Sheela Patel (SPARC)
Sundar Burra (SPARC)

Photo:
Pavement dwellers, Byculla, Mumbai

© Patrick Wakely

Case Study 5: INDIA

Counting the invisible: The census of pavement dwellers in Mumbai

This case shows how, from a joint investigation on pavement dwellers in the city of Mumbai, the NGO Society for the Promotion of Area Resource Centres (SPARC) together with Mahila Milan (Women Together), an organization of women pavement dwellers, and the National Slum Dwellers Federation developed an approach to gathering information in the form of socio-economic statistics and life histories, which proved crucial in helping them improve their situation. This led to the creation of an information base on the pavement dwellers and established within SPARC and its partners new ways of creating knowledge in partnership with people.

Pavement dwellers are among the poorest and the most vulnerable urban dwellers in India. Most have no choice but to live on the pavements because of the high cost and low availability of formal housing, especially in cities such as Mumbai, and the fact that they cannot afford public transport and thus need to live at a short distance from places where they can get work. They face constant threats of having their homes demolished and their valuables confiscated. Most are refused access to ration cards since they have no permanent address and they lack the income to supply themselves with food and fuel on a daily basis.

SPARC started its work in the area of Mumbai with the largest concentration of pavement families. The NGO established the Byculla Area Resource Centre. This provided women pavement dwellers with a space where they could meet and discuss their experiences and perspectives. The women explored ways to break their isolation from the rest of the city and improve their situation. One of the first strategies they elaborated was the organization of an enumeration of the pavement families living in the Byculla area in 1985. At that point, the most up-to-date official census only counted registered households and slum dwellers but ignored the pavement dwellers, thus effectively excluding them from the arena of public policy and service provision.

The survey involved pavement dwellers who had organized themselves in groups and communities with support from SPARC and the help of trained personnel. It covered over 6,000 households, accounting for nearly 27,000 people. The results and findings, which were published by SPARC, enabled pavement dwellers to be formally recognized and visible to the authorities and the rest of the city. The information helped to improve awareness of the pavement dwellers, their needs and conditions. It set the advocacy base for policy change in favour of the urban poor and the official recognition of pavement dwellers.

The enumeration additionally improved self-confidence within pavement dweller communities. Before the census, pavement dwellers had typically formed support networks on the basis kinship, ethnicity, language, geographical origin and so on. The census created a new, parallel identity, helping pavement dwellers to feel part of the larger community of the urban poor.

Community-led censuses and surveys have today become one of the main strategies promoted by SPARC and their partners for community mobilization and public advocacy. They have proved an important tool for building communities' capacity to articulate their knowledge on their own situation and the situation of those with whom they interact. They have been crucial in initiating and sustaining effective processes of poverty alleviation in urban areas.

There are real skills involved in even beginning to understand the extent, needs and values of highly marginalized groups such as the pavement dwellers in Case Study 5. Orthodox surveys are unlikely to expose them. Keeping a low profile is often a survival strategy for poor urban communities. Officialdom is experienced as a threat to their livelihoods and aspirations rather than a support. Suspicion and hostility discourages cooperation with and by those in authority from outside the community.

Gaining the confidence of people normally excluded or harassed by official agencies takes time and skill and may well depend on introductions provided by intermediaries. Area resource centres, and similar institutions, can be valuable nodes giving entry to local networks. Crucially though, information collection, analysis and dissemination has to be for the benefit of those providing the information; this requires a rather different mindset than the conventional outlook of many researchers and data collectors.

Contacts:
SPARC
PO Box 9389
Mumbai 400 026
India
Tel: +91 22 2386 5053 /
+91 22 2385 8785
Fax: +91 22 2388 7566
e-mail:
admin@sparcindia.org /
sparc@vsnl.in

3.4 Understanding the cultural dimensions

Culture is increasingly recognized as the fourth dimension of sustainable development, alongside the environment, the economy and social equity. The built and natural environment is a product of cultures and an important part of identity. Yet too often officialdom is blind to the diversity of cultures that exist in an area and their potential to enrich and broaden appreciation of a place.

In the Who We Are project described in Case Study 6, ethnic minority groups in a town in the United Kingdom were able to find ways to share and celebrate their different experiences and cultures

Case Study 6: UK

Including minority ethnic communities' views and heritage in the built and natural environment

Immigrant minority ethnic communities' cultural heritage is not commonly well understood by the host society. Lack of awareness of different cultures can easily become self-perpetuating; orthodox approaches understand heritage only in terms of the majority community, so minorities feel their heritage is not a part of planning for heritage conservation, and so do not get involved, with the result that decision makers and planners remain ignorant of differences in cultural heritage.

Further information:

Who We Are project
website:
http://www.whoweare.org.uk
Black Environmental Network
website: www.ben-
network.org.uk

Sources:

Pam Green (BEN)
Mike Cherry (BEN)

Contact:

Pam Green
Black Environment Network
(UK Office)
60 High Street
Llanberis, Gwynedd
LL55 4EU

Tel/Fax: 01286 870715
e-mail: ukoffice@ben-
network.org.uk

In Swansea, the Black Environment Network (BEN) tackled this problem by working with African, Bangladeshi, Chinese, Filipino and Iraqi communities to gather information about their past, present and future in relation to where they live and the surrounding countryside of South Wales. The Who We Are project focused on stories of life and family history in the five countries of origin, aspects of living in Swansea today, the ways these communities contribute to the look and feel of the city, and their visions for Swansea's culturally diverse future. It created an opportunity for these ethnic communities to celebrate their past as part of the city's history, and to suggest ideas for improvements to Swansea's buildings and natural environment.

Their work was supported by the Balchder Bro scheme (Welsh phrase for 'Pride of Place') – a two-year pilot project implemented in Wales to enable communities to protect and enhance their heritage. BEN developed a series of workshops to encourage communities to consider what was distinctive about their local environment and heritage and motivate others to appreciate and care for it. People shared photos and created audio recordings and text aimed at capturing and celebrating their ideas, skills and opinions. These were used to create a website in order to share aspects of cultural heritage with the wider community and to inform community planners, local authorities and other mainstream organizations about how to assist minority communities in realizing their vision for the city's future.

Within a year, more than a hundred people took an active part in the project. In the longer term, BEN hopes to raise funds to employ a part-time worker from within the ethnic communities to build on the Who We Are project and encourage other communities to develop their own web pages and celebrate their unique cultural heritage and contribution to the future of their local built and natural environment.

The organization of workshops around diverse events, ranging from community festivals to picnics in the park, is a good way to bring together people from different communities, and train them in consultation skills so they can themselves conduct workshops within their own communities. People display genuine pride in their heritage and are keen to participate, sharing stories about their backgrounds. This is well reflected through the lively Who We Are website, which offers a variety of links to learn more about different ethnic festivals and customs, discover communities' contributions to their built and natural environment, or download recipes and songs. A key skill in the implementation of such multicultural projects is the coordination efforts required to oversee the facilitation of workshops and the management of content uploaded to the website.

The project has allowed a formerly marginalized section of Swansea's population to suggest improvements they would like to see in their urban environment. For example, one person from the Bangladeshi community describes on the website the contrast between a very peaceful village back home with bamboo buildings, and the rather dull buildings and unsafe streets in some parts of present-day Swansea. She dreams of a cleaner city with fewer cars, more trees and safer places for women. Who We Are also provides a map of the area indicating the high points and low points in the built and natural environment, as identified by workshop participants. Ethnic communities are pleased when mainstream organizations show an interest in their culture. It builds confidence and feelings of inclusion, as they are able to make their voices heard for the future of their community and living environment.

3.5 Summary

Information and understanding is always a pre-requisite for effective planning. However, collecting information takes time and is expensive, so there is a balance to be struck. Making such judgements is itself a skill. This chapter has also shown that information handling is not just a technical matter; information is power, and too often the conventional information sources that are most readily available to those making urban plans and strategies fail to recognize the poor.

The case studies here show how collaborations with poor and/or traditionally marginalized groups can have multiple benefits. New information and understanding is generated in a cost-effective manner. This is then the basis for better outcomes that more fairly reflect the needs of the poor and respect the environment, while also gaining consent and working with, rather than against, market actors and the private sector. The process of collaboration and sharing information and analysis is also empowering and builds new skills and confidence among all those involved; it creates a platform for further dialogue.

Key messages

☐ **New information can reveal new potentials.**

☐ **Collaboration and networking to gather and analyze information and to share understandings are not just technical matters, they are means of empowerment and capacity building.**

☐ **New skills and attitudes are needed to reach new sources of information and understanding. These include skills in identifying stakeholders, understanding the nature of livelihoods, of markets, of natural resources, and of different cultures.**

☐ **These skills can be applied at all scales, from a site to a continent.**

4 Communication, negotiation and inclusion

There are few, if any, countries today where planners can impose their blueprints on others. However, plans remain necessary as means to coordinate the actions of separate actors and agencies involved in development. Therefore plans need to be produced through a process of communication and negotiation. In some situations the role of a planner may even be that of mediating independently between parties to a dispute. This is why skills of communication, negotiation and mediation are so important.

Settlements are home to a highly diverse range of people and communities. There is no unambiguous voice speaking for 'the public interest' in the way models of public policy making once assumed. There is a multitude of voices among city dwellers, yet, as has been argued in Chapter 3, the voices of the poor have often been unheard, despite the fact that the needs of the poor are seen to be central to the process of sustainable development.

There are huge challenges here that become ever more acute in conditions of rapid urbanization and the urbanization of poverty. These involve constructing ways for different stakeholders to validate claims, identify priorities and develop strategies collectively through interaction and debate, while creating the mechanisms for inclusion of differently empowered social groups. There is a huge skills gap in this topic that a chapter such as this cannot possibly fill. However, it can point to some of the skills that are being used, and show again that creativ e approaches are possible and can produce better outcomes than past routines.

4.1 Participate, communicate, interact

Planners, among other development-related professionals, are central to the interactive processes of participatory urban development. They are in a position to contribute knowledge and analytical skills to the process and, with the right understanding, to coordinate exchange processes. This requires an ability to set and maintain alliances through building capacity among other stakeholders in a politically sensitive manner, and promote a sense of a shared vision. It demands a capacity to listen and understand others' points of view (and the ways these views are expressed), as well as good communication and presentation skills.

Post-apartheid South African illustrates these dilemmas in an extreme form. A planning system that had been central to the segregation of people that was the heart of apartheid, had to be restructured quickly for the new democracy. Areas suffering from deep rural poverty had simply had no local government. One of the tools developed to create a new platform for economic development and fairer service delivery was Integrated Development Plans (IDPs). Not surprisingly there has been considerable debate about how effective these have been. Case study 7 looks at the participatory process of preparing the eNondakusuka Municipality Integrated Development Plan. It shows skills of developing consensus among local residents through communication, mutual listening and debate. It demonstrates how, despite the post-apartheid social schisms of South African cities, an institutional capacity to collaborate and coordinate priorities for action can be built up.

Case Study 7: SOUTH AFRICA

Debating Integrated Development Plans across a local authority

In 2000, a new form of local government was instituted in South Africa, changing the role of local authorities from one with limited service provision and regulatory powers to a broad developmental function. A key part of this was the planning of development at local level through IDPs, which are essentially oriented to identifying local development needs and potential and relating these to the management, budgeting and planning functions of local authorities. Every municipality in South Africa is required to produce five-year strategic plans that are reviewed annually in consultation with communities and stakeholders. The plans seek to promote integration by balancing social, economic and ecological pillars of sustainability and coordinating actions across sectors and spheres of government. They must contain a vision for the development of the municipal area, and development objectives, strategies, projects and programmes.

The preparation process of the IDP is not seen as a one-off planning exercise, but is rather the start of a new process of strategic local government. IDPs bridge and integrate: equal spheres of government (vertical coordination); sectors (horizontal coordination); urban and rural, non-tribal and tribal areas; and overcome historic racial divisions and inequalities. Another key challenge is about building social inclusion in a diverse cultural context with a developmental objective and balancing basic economic priorities between local needs and strategic opportunities. The issue of social inclusion is of particular importance given the deep social rifts and functional dislocation inherited from the apartheid past.

eNdondakusuka, Kwa-Zulu Natal, is a new municipality formed after the local government demarcation process in 2000. The IDP process commenced in December 2001. It was important that the newly and democratically elected representatives were sufficiently empowered to facilitate community awareness at ward level. In addition, it was considered necessary to ensure non-political engagement, so advertisements were placed in the local press calling for interested parties to register for representation on the statutory Representative Forum. A total of 109 organizations representing social groups, civic associations and economic interest groups, from organized labour and residents associations to sport and drama groups, registered. Key stakeholders who had not necessarily responded were further identified and invited to attend all workshops and meetings.

The two Representative Forum meetings and seven sectoral workshops elicited very positive interest. Approximately 600 people attended, with representation from all sectors of the local community. Participants were encouraged to speak out and express their views on the topics addressed. The final outcome was a list of priority issues to be addressed by the IDP. Rather than a list of compiled wishes, this was a prioritized list of real

© Christine Platt

Photo:
Juxtaposition of the formal housing and informal settlement in eNdondakusuka

Further information:

A Guide to Integrated Development Planning for Local Government in South Africa, http://www.etu.org.za/toolbox/docs/localgov/webidp.html

OPDM (2003) Participatory Planning for Sustainable Communities: International Experience in Mediation, Negotiation and Engagement in Making Plans, Office of the British Deputy Prime Minister, London

Source:

Christine Platt

Contact:

Christine Platt
President
The South African Planning Institute (SAPI)
PO Box 12381
BENORYN
1504
Tel/Fax: 011-425-4502
e-mail: plattch@mweb.co.za

concerns, which had been discussed, debated and agreed on (or at least accepted) by all community representatives during the workshops. The workshops were facilitated by the local authority's planner together with a professional Zulu speaking facilitator, where necessary. It was imperative that all participants felt free to use whichever language they felt most comfortable with. Another important point was that nothing had been written prior to the workshops and there were no prior positions for the local authority or the planner to defend.

The draft proposals were considered in another workshop with the elected councillors and officials. The final IDP document was then advertised for public comment before being presented at a final Representative Forum meeting. There was facilitation by a consultant planner throughout the IDP preparation process to ensure that issues raised were translated into strategies that were achievable given the limited resources of the eNdondakusuka municipality. Any issue raised was tested to see if the problem was shared among the broader community. There were also instances where the community was happy to accept that there were specific concerns coming from a particular group that had merit and needed to be recorded as a priority of the community in its broadest sense.

The fact that the negotiation and mediation of the plan was done at the local authority scale with all participants hearing the points raised by each other was critical to the coherence, legitimacy and feasibility of the IDP. Preparation of smaller scale local area plans by, for example, ward level groups, would have made the task of marrying competing demands at a later stage difficult, if not impossible. Moreover, preparing plans through mutual listening enabled people to hear one another's concerns and to understand better the needs and interests within the broader community. Officials learned by hearing how the community as whole responded regarding competing needs. Many participants expressed how they had learnt from, and about, one another in the process: 'protest has been changed into development'.

The case of the eNdondakusuka IDP is notable for the success achieved in building consensus among diverse groups in a very short space of time and with very limited use of professional staff resources. The participatory processes have been successfully sustained through IDP reviews. The system of Representative Forum meetings coupled with community-based sectoral workshops has been continued over the past four years and, critically, the understanding shown by the community at the start of the IDP process about the limitations and reality of development in a resource-poor municipality has been sustained. The 2002 IDP has now reached the end of its life, following the recent local authority elections, and at the last Representative Forum meeting, community representatives expressed their satisfaction at the degree to which the priority issues agreed with the community in 2002 had been addressed by the municipality.

This case study shows the use of a number of skills. There are skills of working with politicians and local representatives so that they have a sense of ownership of the process, but accept that ownership does not mean monopoly. As these politicians were largely serving their first term in public office, there was an element of capacity building for elected members also. Skills of outreach and understanding of diversity were needed to bring 109 organizations into the IDP process. Again this process of involvement was also a process of capacity building, but the learning was two-way, for the consultant doing this work was also breaking new ground and learning from the process.

Listening skills are clearly very important in a situation such as the one in eNdondakusuka, which also shows how a relatively simple institution such as a Representative Forum can be a successful means of working together. The example also points up the importance of language skills. The solution in this case was a Zulu-speaking facilitator, but language is an important skill for planners or other officials in situations where the language of the people they are serving is not their own language. The increasing diversity of settlements means this issue is likely to become more common.

4.2 Negotiation, mediation and conflict resolution

Plans are necessary because there are conflicts of interest in the development of settlements and regions. Skills for understanding and resolving conflicts are therefore core planning skills. Such skills have received surprisingly little attention, though to some degree they have to be learned to do the job.

Possibilities of consensus emerge from reflective discussions of conflicting interests and needs. Planners and related professionals must develop the skills to manage conflicts and enable negotiated consensus around key development issues. Such skills include: the capacity to anticipate potential conflicts of interest and recognize the key issues quickly; an open attitude, with the willingness to compromise and solve problems; patience and stamina; flexibility to tolerate conflict and stress; excellent listening skills and sensitivity to the needs of others; the readiness to question conventional planning rationalism and expertise, as well as an ability to cope with personal attack or abuse.

Negotiation, mediation and conflict resolution are less about taking risks than carefully evaluating risks and being able to plan and time a strategy in order to take the best decisions possible in uncertain situations. Effective negotiation, moreover, demands some practice and feedback. It involves preparation, proactive strategies and a good knowledge of one's own strengths and weaknesses. Below are examples of the type of questions one needs to ask in the preparation of a negotiation process*

*Adapted from Thomson, L. (2000) The Mind and Heart of the Negotiator, Prentice Hall, NJ; and Carter, W. (1991) Negotiating Skills: Participant's Guide, Harbridge Consulting Group Ltd, New York.

Self - Assesment
- ☐ What do I want?
- ☐ What do I really need? What is my target or objective?
- ☐ What are the priorities of needs and wants?
- ☐ What am I willing to sacrifice in exchange?
- ☐ What are my pressures, limits or constraining factors?
- ☐ What is my best alternative to a negotiated agreement – i.e. the point at which I would walk away?

Assessment of the other parties
- ☐ Who are they?
- ☐ What do they want? Do they all share the same objective or interests?
- ☐ What do they really need? What is their target?
- ☐ What are the priorities of needs and wants?
- ☐ What are they willing to sacrifice in exchange?
- ☐ What are their pressures, limits or constraining factors?

Possible conflicts
- ☐ What are the possible conflicts?
- ☐ Do you understand where conflict might occur?
- ☐ What are the positions between the target and the best alternative to a negotiated agreement?
- ☐ How much leeway will you allow yourself?
- ☐ How will you try to resolve points of conflict (vary offer? Call on mediator or arbitrator?)?

Case Study 8, from Bangladesh, illustrates how a successful negotiation process can lead to urban utility reform in favour of the urban poor. In this example, social intermediation by the NGO Dushtha Shasthya Kendra (DSK) played a key role in facilitating negotiation for providing slum communities with municipal water provision. The DSK model also demonstrates how, with the right balance of diplomacy and political force, it is possible for an NGO or organized community groups to navigate between the red tape and power struggles imposed by government authorities and other stakeholders and progressively gain confidence through the setting of successful precedents. Another way to contain conflicts is to agree and stick to a set of rules.

Case Study 8: BANGLADESH

Negotiating water connection for the urban poor

A local NGO, Dushtha Shasthya Kendra has helped residents of some of Dhaka's squatter settlements gain access to public water and sanitation services. In Dhaka, the agency responsible for water provision, the Dhaka Water Supply and Sewerage Authority (DWASA), is mandated to provide connections only to households who can demonstrate legal tenure of their plot. This effectively excludes the large majority of slum dwellers. Persuading DWASA to install water points in squatter neighbourhoods was an important breakthrough that demanded many years and efforts of negotiation as well as important skills to gradually build the confidence among stakeholders that ways exist for informal communities to access formal utility services with a win-win outcome.

© WaterAid

DSK had been working among the slum and squatter neighbourhoods of Dhaka for several years when it undertook to act as an intermediary between slum communities and the public water authority to enable the establishment of water connections in some of Dhaka slums. When slum communities expressed their willingness to pay for water supply services, DSK offered the municipal water authority the opportunity to serve as guarantor on their behalf for the security deposit and the regular payment of bills. DWASA officials eventually agreed to waive their usual policy and approved two water points in poor settlements of Dhaka, in 1992 and 1994.

Based on its experience with its first initiatives, DSK then worked at developing a replicable model for sustainable water supply for the urban poor. They managed to negotiate with DWASA the launching of a pilot project in 12 slum communities, provided that the cost for delivering the services would be recovered within the existing institutional framework. They successfully obtained permission from Dhaka City Corporation (DCC) to build water points and to cut roads on lands owned by DCC. The UNDP-World Bank Water and Sanitation Programme, the Swiss Agency for Development and Co-operation and the international NGO WaterAid provided technical support, as well as the initial funds in the form of kick-off loans.

The objectives were to build bridges between the water utility agency and potential user communities through advocacy and intermediation and encourage changes in the local institutional environment to facilitate the supply of water to the urban poor. In parallel, DSK helped community groups to mobilize and organize themselves in management committees for the water points and latrines. This included building their capacity to manage the water points and ensure prompt and regular payment of water bills, and meet supervision and maintenance costs, as well as repaying the capital cost. DSK also provided them with technical assistance to establish and maintain water connections as well as ancillary facilities. Dr Dibalok Singha of DSK explains 'the challenge was to

Further information:
Akash, M. M. and Singha, D. (2003) Provision of Water Points in Low Income Communities in Dhaka, Bangladesh, paper prepared for the Civil Society Consultation of the 2003 Commonwealth Finance Ministers Meeting, Bandar Seri Begawan, Brunei Darussalam, 22–24 July, Commonwealth Foundation, London
Matin, N. (1999) 'Social intermediation: Towards gaining access to water for squatter communities in Dhaka', Water for All Series (May), Asian Development Bank
Rokeya, A. (2003) DSK: A Model for Securing Access to Water for the Urban Poor, WaterAid Fieldwork Report, WaterAid, London
Singha, D. (2001) Social Intermediation for the Urban Poor in Bangladesh: Facilitating Dialogue between Stakeholders and Change of Practice to Ensure Legal Access to Basic Water, Sanitation and Hygiene Education Services for Slum Communities, paper presented at the DFID Regional Livelihoods Workshop: Reaching the Poor in Asia, 8–10 May, DFID, London

Source:
Timeyin Uwejamomere (WaterAid UK)
Ziaul Kabir (WaterAid Bangladesh)

© WaterAid

Contacts:
DSK – Dushtha Shasthya
Kendra
4/8 Iqbal Road
Block-A,
Mohammadpur
Dhaka-1207
Bangladesh
Tel/Fax: 9128520 / 8115764
Dr. Dibalok Singha
Executive Director
e-mail: dsk@citechco.net /
dskhq@citechco.net
WaterAid Bangladesh
House 97/B, Road 25,
Block-A, Banani,
Dhaka – 1213,
Bangladesh.
Tel: 880 2 8815757, 8818521
Fax: 880 2 8818521
Ziaul Kabir
Programme Officer -
Advocacy
e-mail:
ziaul@wateraidbd.org
WaterAid UK
2nd floor
47–49 Durham Street
London, SE11 5JD
United Kingdom
Tel: +44 20 7793 4500
Fax: +44 20 7793 4545
Website:
wateraid@wateraid.org
Timeyin Uwejamomere
Policy Officer, Urban W&S
Services
e-mail:
TimeyinUwejamomere@wat
eraid.org

demonstrate and prove that such initiatives are successful; and on the strength of such experience to influence and push local governments to make real investments in such projects to the benefit of the depressed target groups'.

The water delivery model developed by DSK in Dhaka has proven to city authorities that when they are willing to pay, informal communities can be capable and responsible managers of essential services, as well as reliable clients for the relevant service providers. For DWASA, this represents an effective system for regularization of illegal connections and corresponding increased revenue. Moreover, equity of supply to the urban poor can be viewed as politically rewarding for those local government officials who have been supporting the programme. Since the inception of the project in 1996, DWASA has become increasingly confident in extending its service facilities to slums and squatter settlements. 88 water points have been established in 70 slum areas, benefiting more than 200,000 people, whilst about 12 water points have been paid for and handed over to user groups. The project's success in showing the potential for informal communities to be reliable clients has prompted the water authority to allow communities to apply for water connections on their own behalf without the need for a guarantor. The water authority is also cooperating in the replication of the project in 110 community-managed water systems, benefiting around 60,000 slum dwellers, with plans to expand the arrangement to one of the largest slums in the city with over 250,000 inhabitants.

Gradually, DSK hopes to transfer responsibilities to communities themselves, including approaching and negotiating with DWASA and DCC. Introducing the communities to these agencies may help establish their right to water and sanitation services. Indeed, the initial years of careful but persistent negotiation through the setting of successful precedents have induced a change of mindset in the Dhaka authorities and utilities. It has also brought about significant changes in power relationships between slum dwellers, landlords, the water utility and city authorities. Dr Singha acknowledges that working with official bodies such as DWASA or DCC takes time 'but slowly and surely acceptance is reached'. Clearly, this depends on the commitment of senior managers in these key agencies, but it is also essential that field-level officials be willing to cooperate in the initiative. Influence from outside agencies and international organizations is also a major factor to help convince sceptics within local authorities and utilities.

The model has started a new wave of thinking and, in close association with WaterAid, has been replicated to scale with other NGOs and municipal authorities throughout the country. Lessons from the model have also encouraged the draft final Dhaka Water Supply Policy to include community participation as a policy priority, mentioning that communities will provide suggestions for better services and help raise awareness of stakeholders on the water policy, as well as monitor the implementation of government policy and plans. The policy furthermore commits to ensuring full water supply coverage to the urban poor of Dhaka's slums. More than a successful negotiation experience, the DSK model also proved an effective entry point for urban utility reform in favour of the urban poor.

This case study shows how dramatic the benefits of a successful negotiation can be. It also reveals the importance of mindsets and perceptions in any negotiation. One of the skills involved in negotiation is the ability to grasp the mindsets of the different parties and to appreciate what information is needed to overcome presumptions and prejudices that are barriers to agreement. Building confidence and mutual respect between the different parties to the negotiation is essential to getting agreement. In the case study it meant convincing the water authority that squatters could be reliable clients. Information is important in this process, a theme already demonstrated in Chapter 3. It is also important to try to identify and work towards outcomes in which all parties gain something.

Case Study 9, from Malawi, again shows how negotiations verging on mediation through the work of an NGO were able to bridge the gap between the 'normal' policies of a local authority and the needs of the urban poor. By negotiating a compromise solution that was then shown to work, new confidences were developed. This then enabled the project to be scaled up and the lessons and benefits spread to other areas of the city.

Case Study 9: MALAWI

Analyzing problems and opportunities to determine a path to better housing for the urban poor

Cities in Malawi, now one of the most rapidly urbanizing countries in the world, are ill-equipped to deal with the growing number of people flooding its urban centres. Newcomers, including a growing number of refugees, are forced to live in informal and overcrowded settlements characterized by inadequate housing, hazardous health conditions, a serious lack of water supply and sanitation facilities, and limited access to health, education, security and other public services.

The Malawi Homeless People's Federation (MHPF) emerged from the regrouping of community savings groups active in slum areas of the capital city Lilongwe in early 2003. The Malawi Federation are now active in every informal settlement in Lilongwe and Blantyre, with a total membership of nearly 30,000 people. Besides organizing and managing group savings schemes, which operate on a daily basis in slum communities with the aim of improving living conditions, the Malawian Federation has taken the lead in settlement upgrading by identifying problems and actively pursuing partnerships and solutions. The Centre for Community Organization and Development (CCODE), an NGO that initially helped to link community groups in urban Malawi, supports the Federation by linking it to policy makers, planners and managers in government and local authorities.

In their diagnosis and analysis of Lilongwe's housing problems, community group members felt that the best

© Mtafu A. Zeleza Manda, CCODE

Source:
Mtafu A. Zeleza Manda

Contact:
Sikhulile (Siku) Nkhoma
Director and founder of CCODE
Centre for Community Organisation and Development
Second Floor Nasa House
Area 3, PO Box 2109
Lilongwe , Malawi
Tel:+2651756781/2
Fax: +265 1 756781/2
Mobile: +265 8 864618
e-mail:
skuenkoma@malawi.net

Photo:
Community water point.

Contacts:

Mtafu A. Zeleza Manda
Board Chairman and co-
founder of CCODE
ALMA Consultancy
PO Box 30193, Lilongwe /
Po Box 876, Mzuzu
Malawi
Tel: + 265 1 757 912
Fax : + 265 1 755 073
Mobile : + 265 8 867 752 /
9 30 77 20
e-mail:
mmanda.scdp@malawi.net
mazmanda@yahoo.com

Website:
http://www.sdinet.org/coun
tries/malawi.htm

entry point for the poor to reach out to policy makers and planners was through organization and collective action led by CCODE and the Federation. With CCODE's support, the Federation approached the Lilongwe City Assembly to request land for housing in August of 2004. The Assembly offered the Federation a parcel of land with 99 plots. The number of Federation members in Lilongwe at the time was approximately 400. Therefore, 99 plots were not sufficient. A proposal was made to the City of Lilongwe to allow the Federation members reduce the plot sizes so that they would be as small as possible to accommodate more homes, but also to reduce costs of rates in future. After negotiations, the idea was accepted, the plot sizes were reduced and 222 plots were created.

Due to the success of this initial process and community-managed construction of houses since, Lilongwe City Assembly is today interested in offering more land to the Federation. In Blantyre, the city has offered to assist the Federation in conducting a citywide slum enumeration of about 17 slum communities. City authorities are also finalizing land allocation procedures to the Federation with the Ministry of Lands.

In collaboration with local officials, Lilongwe water board and the private sector, MHPF continues to work to improve and simplify access to clean water and sanitation, identified by Federation members as one of the most pressing issues in urban Malawi. In addition, in July of 2005, CCODE and MHPF signed a memorandum of understanding with the Blantyre City Assembly for the incorporation of MHPF into the city's upgrading strategies within the ongoing UN-HABITAT initiative that aims to make Blantyre a 'City Without Slums' over the next decade.

4.3 Building inclusion

Planning must not only attempt to include all sections of the community but also promote the inclusion of marginalized groups in the society and economy of the city. Planning and interactive processes that 'treat everybody the same' are likely to reproduce and strengthen patterns of inequality and exclusion. Because an important part of deprivation or marginalization is the lack of 'voice' and a sense of social exclusion, and because various parties have varying quality of information, uneven levels of decision making and different negotiation capacities, planners and professionals must acknowledge the relations of power that exist and work in order to counter-balance them in a more equitable way.

The young, the elderly, women, ethnic minorities, the poor, those with disabilities and non-property owners are typically overlooked in public policy discussions. Building their capacity to organize and mobilize around their needs and priorities can help to make their voice heard and redress imbalances in their representation. Planning practice must be aware of the lives and needs of these groups. For example, in many societies, women are less likely to attend late afternoon and evening meetings when they need to prepare food for the evening; in others they cannot attend public events unescorted. Inclusive mechanisms need to respect and value different forms of knowledge and expression. In this way, the use of non-technical language is likely to reduce the barriers for engagement with the public.

The following case studies show practical initiatives that promote a better inclusion of under-represented groups in the local planning process. Through the organization of educational workshops, community surveys, grassroots initiatives or training of community leaders, they built people's capacity to get their needs recognized.

Case Study 10: UK

Building inclusion through the Planning Aid programme

Planning Aid is a voluntary movement supported by the Royal Town Planning Institute (RTPI) that aims to empower local communities to effectively engage with the planning process and influence decisions affecting their areas. Planning Aid provides free and independent professional planning advice to groups and individuals who do not have the means to employ professional planning experts. The service carries out a range of outreach, education and community capacity-building projects and delivers initiatives involving people in the formulation of planning policy and in schemes to improve their areas. Strong partnerships with other bodies at national, regional and local levels have been developed to assert this agenda. This includes working with national planning and regeneration bodies, regional assemblies, local authorities, schools and regional development agencies.

The range of skills and the expertise of Planning Aid staff and volunteers enable it to deliver a high-quality service for which there is a clear public demand. A regional structure consisting of 13 offices throughout England, Wales, Scotland and Northern Ireland makes the service responsive to the needs of local communities, helping it to deliver sustainable communities and contribute to local democracy.

Planning Aid for London's contributions between 2004 and 2005 include helping 62 community organizations to deepen their involvement in the redevelopment of a large area of industrial and railway wasteland in central London (King's Cross). Planning Aid workers led a series of workshops and consultations with these groups to expand their understanding of the local authority (Camden Borough) and developers' documents outlining proposals for change in the area. Documents on the redevelopment plans posed significant difficulties for community groups because of their technical complexity and vagueness in terms of how mixed-use areas would be utilized. An additional challenge for Planning Aid's efforts was the extremely diverse composition of this part of London in terms of ethnicity, ability and above average levels of homelessness and drug abuse.

After initial meetings with the King's Cross Forum and time analyzing the 12 planning documents and approximately 30 supporting documents, Planning Aid provided the 62 groups involved in the King's Cross Forum with more simply-worded summaries of official documents. This led to subsequent steps where legalities were discussed, strategies were analyzed and specific issues for a response were identified and prioritized. The Forum's response influenced a revised proposal from the developer. Planning Aid worked with community groups to assess this second proposal and 'grade' it in terms of how it addressed earlier points raised by the community.

Source:
Carol Ryall

Contact:
Carol Ryall
Planning Aid for London
Unit 2, 11–29 Fashion Street
London E1 6PX

Tel: +44 (0)20 7247 4900
e-mail: info@planningaidfor-london.org.uk
Website:
http://www.planningaid.rtpi.org.uk/

> Significant in terms of Planning Aid for London's short- and long-term contributions to the King's Cross redevelopment was the way in which its workers mediated between the community forum and the local council, which held ultimate control over development decisions. The Planning Aid volunteers had to gain the trust of many groups with disparate interests, ensure that no groups dominated or were pushed aside, and deal with intense emotions. Planning Aid sought specialist help when needed and distributed information to as wide a range of people as possible by using local translators. Planning Aid for London helped the Forum to learn more about the development, particularly the issues of most concern to them.

One key point to make from this case study is the fact that Planning Aid exists because there are professional planners who are prepared to give their time and expertise for free to help those who cannot afford to hire consultants to advise them. This may not be a skill but it is certainly an important attitude and aspect of professionalism in building more inclusive forms of planning.

Among the skills demonstrated in the Kings Cross example are running workshops, and decoding technical documents and communicating their meaning to diverse audiences. The former demands good organizational skills – successful workshops do not just happen. The latter is very important, and involves analytical abilities and understanding but also skills in synthesis and summarizing. Skills in networking and building confidence among very different groups and agencies are also central to the practice of the Planning Aid volunteers. While communication skills infuse all aspects of this example, it also shows aspects of mediation in the ability to help the 62 different groups find ways forward.

The importance of gender as a factor in development has been increasingly recognized. Our next case study shows how the dissemination of information, including the use of seminars with city officials and other stakeholders can promote the role of women and their concerns in policy and institutions. Planning that is better informed of the needs and views of all the local population is better planning. People who know they are being listened to gain confidence and a stronger sense of belonging to their local community.

Case Stusy 11: RUSSIA

Mainstreaming gender into the local policy agenda

The Information Centre of the Independent Women's Forum (ICIWF) is a non-profit organization founded in 1994, networking women's organizations and now active throughout Russia and the Commonwealth of Independent States (CIS). The Centre disseminates information on women's rights and gender issues, encourages concerted actions among women's organizations, exchanges information through forums and e-mails with women's organizations across the CIS, supports women's grassroots initiatives, and organizes educational projects, all with the aim of promoting less-discriminatory societies, and establishing a strong position for women and their concerns in policy and institutions.

The Centre is using the Habitat Agenda (which calls for the promotion of gender equality in human settlement development) through the Women's Network for the Habitat Agenda Promotion to foster the mainstreaming of gender issues into urban, municipal and local policy. At national level, the ICIWF draws from its established partnership with a range of government ministries to transfer information between the federal and the local levels, and advocate to the State Duma (parliament) on behalf of grassroots organizations. With its large panel of projects and activities in different locations across Russia and the CIS, ICIWF is demonstrating that gender equity can be incorporated into the wider agenda of sustainability.

© ICIWF

Photo:
New social skill training with NGO and police

Further information:
The ICIWF issues a newsletter Vestnik in Russian, downloadable from the internet at http://www.owl.ru/win/women/org001/v21.htm

Source:
Elizaveta Bozhoka

Contact:
Elizaveta Bozhkova
ICIWF
p/b 230 Moscow 119019, Russia
Tel/Fax: +7-(495)366-92-74
e-mail: iciwf@okb-telecom.net
Website:
http://www.owl.ru/win/women/org001

With experience, ICIWF has worked out its own approach and methods based on the building of partnerships, sharing experience and information, and cooperation with the relevant local authorities. Women's safety is an important concern, and experience suggests the issues are best addressed through the mobilization of neighbourhood groups or local communities. Moreover, housing and communal reforms in Russia are based on local groups joining together within a certain territory. However, this culture of dialogue is often lacking. People living in large housing blocks often do not know each other and 'have no common language'. ICIWF and its member organizations thus put considerable effort into promoting dialogue and the development of social skills among neighbours, and their mobilization into groups through the organization of joint discussions, training and local development projects. They ensure that residents, and first of all women, take an active part in the planning and implementation of these projects.

Once communities within a neighbourhood are better organized and ready to undertake joint action, the next step is to build the partnership between women's NGOs, neighbourhood communities and the relevant city authorities. This is done through training and seminars involving representatives of the municipal administration, council deputies and the police, as well as neighbourhood and community leaders, women's NGOs, crisis centres and citizens. For example, in Petrozavodsk since October 2003, the ICIWF has organized a series of seminars and training for the city administration, the local police department and the architecture department on how to improve safety levels in the locality or how to render the living environment more women and children friendly. Participatory skills and methods are put forward as procedures for discussion and decision making, as well as for the control and outcome assessment processes.

In parallel, women's groups and their leaders receive training to help them improve their status and promote women's agenda into policy discussions at the municipal and regional levels. The Centre also encourages the publication of articles and information in the local press to make the projects and the problems they are aiming to solve better understood by the public. By December 2003 in Petrozavodsk, the head of the women's group had been invited by the head of the city police department to join the 'Public Advisers', and some women members were given the right to observe the safety of their locality with a specific police identification pass. Meanwhile, the general level of safety in Petrozavodsk's neighbourhoods has improved as people have become more eager to communicate, support each other and participate in crime prevention solutions. The seminars were used to inform joint projects on 'Local Dialogue' and 'Safer Territory', which also included components for improving local plans and architectural designs according to safety and gender-friendly criteria. According to the figures of the Petrozavodsk Police Department, the number of crimes has significantly decreased in these districts. Domestic violence has also reduced. The partnership between women's groups and the police contributed to changing behaviours and stereotypes among police staff and citizens, and raised public awareness on gender and safety issues.

Mainstreaming is an important concept. It means moving a concern, for example, in the case study for gender issues, from being the focus of interest for just a part of the service, to the mainstream of that service, something that everybody takes seriously and has to factor into their everyday practice. Despite all the examples in these case studies, there is still a long way to go before understanding of diversity and concerns for equal opportunities and before the inclusion of the poor and marginalized are mainstreamed into planning practice globally.

4.4 Summary

Communication, negotiation and inclusion, the themes of this chapter, underpin the understanding of planning and the roles of professionals, as presented in this compendium. They were touched upon in Chapter 3 and will reappear in later chapters. The reason why they are so important is that the planning of settlements is always a process at the interface between different interests, groups and priorities. Confidences have to be built, understandings gained and ideas explored with a myriad of stakeholders. The skills involved are primarily management skills. They include:

- □ Being clear about aims;
- □ Organizing and preparing well;
- □ Managing resources (financial, human and time);
- □ Delivering within time constraints;
- □ Keeping the process moving; not getting side-tracked;
- □ Knowing how to make people feel comfortable and being able to create the right environment for discussion;
- □ Being able to use interactive techniques to stimulate new ideas – not just talking to people;
- □ Accurately recording outcomes and agreements;
- □ Being able to convert agreements into implementation on the ground, and then to scale up successes.

Understanding is also critical. Listening is vital to gain understanding, as is learning from experience. What do people mean? Sometimes it helps to reframe statements so as to clarify the values and priorities. There are always hidden agendas. One of the best ways of revealing them is to ask leading questions – questions that confront things that people have not been willing to talk about. Group dynamics are also important. Who are the leaders and how do they lead? Where are the tensions in the group? How representative are those who speak on behalf of others and what is the basis for their legitimacy?

Key messages

- ☐ Listen, question, synthesize, summarize and look for solutions.

- ☐ Such skills are easily taken for granted; they should be learned and practiced.

5 Being Strategic

The word 'strategic' appears often in development plans, research papers and organizational mission statements. Being strategic is crucial to a planner's work, but what does 'being strategic' actually mean in terms of practical skills in planning?

Being strategic is not the same as planning at a particular scale, such as a city region. Strategic actions are based on an awareness of the complexity of achieving win-win situations and can be at any spatial scale. Being strategic means using problems and opportunities to create power and opening new opportunities where they did not exist before. Strategic interventions must be collective and inclusive, critical and moral. The results of strategic actions under these pretexts are not to be judged in terms of their successes or failures and winners and losers, but rather, in terms of their capacity to facilitate significant and lasting change.

It is the nature of urban change today that puts a premium on being strategic. The issues vary from place to place – adjusting global cities to new knowledge industries, restructuring the fabric and remedying environmental damage in the 'rustbelt' agglomerations of the North, coping somehow with double digit annual demographic increases in towns and cities in the South, or mitigating the hazards posed by climate change in small island states. However disparate the detail, there is a common underlying imperative – the need to act strategically and quickly.

There is at least one other reason why planners need skills in strategic thinking and doing. The previous chapter stressed the importance of seeking agreements in situations of diversity, of helping to build a sense of shared ownership of a project, a programme or a process. This is unlikely to happen if the participants can only see the detail. The bigger picture, the sense of where we are going, why and how to get there, is of fundamental importance to mobilizing human and other resources.

5.1 Strategic action is integrated action

Action designed to make a decisive and lasting difference is likely to be undermined if the actions of other agencies and the market are working against it. In a world where resources are limited, one of the key reasons for, and requirements of, strategic action is to make efficient and effective use of resources that are available by integration. Among the essential skills needed to achieve integration is the ability to see connections and to imagine more than one step at a time.

Case Study 12 shows how integrated and strategic action in a UN-Habitat project in Sri Lanka was able to maximize the underlying benefits of rehabilitation and reconstruction after the 2004 tsunami. In many minds strategic planning is top-down planning, the antithesis of the kind of practices discussed in Chapter 4. The case study presented here shows that being strategic can also work bottom-up and that the human resources of local residents can be vital to a successful strategy.

Case Study 12: SRI LANKA

Post-tsunami reconstruction and rehabilitation in Galle

The tsunami that struck southern Sri Lanka in 2004 resulted in the death or displacement of more than half a million people and the destruction of community infrastructure such as wells, drainage, community centres, preschools, schools and roads. Responding to this disaster, UN-Habitat's Rebuilding Community Infrastructure and Shelter (RCIS) project in Galle focused not only on rebuilding houses but also on supporting communities in the reconstruction of infrastructure. In the 12 months prior to March 2006, the programme assisted 700 households in 10 tsunami-affected communities.

RCIS used a participatory approach that aimed for community-wide impacts through empowering vulnerable people and giving a voice to the tsunami-affected. This included:

☐ The organization of representative bodies to enable communities to take decisions regarding their own rebuilding process;

☐ A key role for target communities in rebuilding essential physical facilities, including shelter, so that they could restart functioning as normal communities;

☐ A livelihood component that encouraged the establishment of small-scale enterprises, c reating wage employment and investment in the rebuilding process as a way of contributing to the recovery of the local economy.

During the process, self-confidence among the beneficiary community has been generated and human dignity restored by fully engaging in the reconstruction those who had suffered but survived the tragedy. Not only were buildings rebuilt, but also shattered lives and communities and self-reliance. Community governance has been re-established as well as self-managed, creating sustainable communities with social facilities and livelihood opportunities.

Source:
Katja Schäfer

Contacts:
Conrad de Tissera, Habitat Programme Manger
UN-Habitat - Colombo, United Nations Human Settlements Programmes
UNDP, 202-204 Bauddhaloka Mawatha
Colombo 7, Sri Lanka
Tel: +94 (0) 11 2580691 Ext: 342
Fax: +94 (0) 11 2581116
e-mail: info@unhabitat.lk, conrad.detissera@undp.org
Website: www.unhabitat.lk

Katja Schäfer, City Planning Officer
UN-Habitat – Hargesia, Somalia
e-mail: katja.schafer@gmail.com

Community Development Councils and Action Plans

As part of the RCIS project's community mobilization activities in the target communities, community development councils (CDCs) were revived, strengthened and, where not in place, established to represent the interests of the wider community. CDCs provided an important institutional link for incorporating community views in Galle's government and helping to implement locally developed Community Action Plans (CAPs), which prioritized needs and identified the actions that would help in addressing these needs. CAPs developed the capacity of communities to take appropriate action for their own development in the framework for the implementation of actions decided on by the communities. Importantly, the identification of needs was not viewed as making a 'wish list' of what communities wanted to be provided as an entitlement, but as a process of understanding their situation and what they needed to do to overcome it in the shortest possible time.

© Katia Schäfer

© Katia Schäfer

© Katia Schäfer

Community Contracting

After a CAP was established with a community, priority areas of assistance were identified and the UN-Habitat Project Office and the CDC of each affected community approved the plan. Subsequently, CDCs, operating as contractors, were in charge of implementing the works according to the agreed schedule of works, specifications, drawings and estimates within an indicated time frame. As the RCIS project promoted cooperation between the different actors in improving the local urban areas, the UN-Habitat Project Office in Galle initially mediated between the different actors. During the course of the project, it withdrew gradually and allowed more room for community decisions and interaction with other partners. In this regard, the RCIS project was a means for empowering communities to take more control of their own lives and seek further assistance not only in reconstructing the tsunami affected physical infrastructure but also in improving their neighbourhoods in the long term.

The communities gained directly from the project implementation through employment as well as through the outputs of the project itself. Furthermore, because community members were directly affected by the way in which the reconstruction work was carried out and because benefits of local contracts went directly back into the community as opposed to an intermediate actor, there was a strong incentive to see that work was carried out properly. Whereas conventional procurement of reconstruction works had a single benefit, the provision of shelter or the infrastructure itself, community partnering doubled the benefits obtained from investment. Physical infrastructure was provided along with skills development and income-generating activities.

Possible employment opportunities arose not only during the implementation of the project, but additionally as small-scale enterprises were created in the community. Through on-the-job training community groups were capable of undertaking tasks of which they had no previous experience. Skilled labour was hired as much as possible from within the community or adjacent areas with residents who were experienced skilled construction workers. These workers played a key role in managing the construction process and had the potential to act as trainers and demonstrators for less experienced individuals.

In being strategic, the RCIS programme has incorporated a learning perspective within a strengthened framework for community input. Displaced residents are guiding the process of reconstruction and learning skills that can be applied in future economic efforts and passed on to other, less-skilled members of the community. While civil society and the private sector are benefiting in terms of increased voice and potential for productiveness and diversification, the public sector, too, has augmented its effectiveness through its commitment to workshops and input through the CDCs. As this example shows, being strategic is about spotting the potential to create 'virtuous circles' where one benefit opens the opportunity to create another. These connected and mutually supportive processes are the essence of sustainable development.

The case study from The Netherlands that follows is an example of integrated strategic action on a different scale and with a very different resource base, though employing similar principles and approaches.

Case Study 13: THE NETHERLANDS

A strategic response to social exclusion and neighbourhood decline

Hoogvleit grew from a small fishing village to become a planned satellite town of Rotterdam during the 1950s and 1960s. It housed about 40,000 people. However, in the 1970s the appartment blocks that had been built became increasingly unpopular and many of the residents who were able to moved out. Those left behind were mainly the poor, immigrant ethnic minorities and single-person households. Industrial closures were followed by high unemployment. The image and reputation of the town, with its nearby harbour and industrial areas, was that of deprivation. Physical isolation from Rotterdam was mirrored by social exclusion, with drugs and crime making the downward spiral worse. Only integrated action at a large scale was likely to turn around the situation in Hoogvleit. This began in 1995 when the local government undertook an extensive exercise to identify the problems. Citizens' involvement was a key component of this stage and those that followed. This led to a major regeneration programme that drew in resources and active support from several important and influential agencies. The municipality of Rotterdam, a powerful big city body, and two of the social housing corporations who owned many of the properties were actively involved, and there was also support from central government. There has been consistent support and complementary policies between the different scales of government involved – key factors for successful strategic action. Furthermore, innovative projects within Hoogvleit have been able to win additional grants and support.

While the key objective was to tackle social exclusion, the regeneration work involved a number of inter-connected and mutually reinforcing strands. These were:

- [ ] improving economic vitality;
- [ ] strengthening social cohesion;
- [ ] sustainability;
- [ ] improvement of the housing stock and living environment;
- [ ] strong civic involvement;
- [ ] area branding (to support and market the positive aspects of the changes the project was delivering).

Further information:
ODPM (2006) UK
Presidency EU Ministerial
Informal on Sustainable
Communities, European
Evidence Review Papers,
Office of the Deputy Prime
Minister, London, pp97–107.
Website: www.wimby.nl

Thus the project is strategic in scale and in its engagement with all aspects of the settlement. The work has involved drastic changes to the physical environment, with substantial levels of demolition and rebuilding. The regeneration plan that came into operation in 1998 will see something like 25 per cent of the housing demolished (over 3,600 dwellings), and the rebuilding of an equivalent number. High quality building is a central part of the plan. The intention is not only to relocate existing residents but to attract new citizens to a place that was previously seen by outsiders as a very unattractive place to live. Effective implementation and delivery are central concerns.

There have also been a number of innovations in housing, including management and marketing and use of environmentally friendly demolition and building processes. A 'Senior Citizens Brigade' has formed through which older people help each other with various problems, including those created by the renewal process itself.

Among the core values in the branding of Hoogvleit are 'self-esteem', 'sense of community and belonging', 'determination' and 'adventure', and one of the results of this was the development of three housing area developments where over 50 people will be living in houses that they designed themselves.

As in the example from Sri Lanka, the need for integrated action and community involvement was firmly grasped in the regeneration of Hoogvleit, though on a different scale and with a different level of resources. Clearly it was not easy to get the various sectoral experts to understand each other's position and expectations. Generic skills were often lacking. One of the housing corporations put together a team of specialists whose skills encompassed project management, process management, communication and civic involvement, policy development and strategy, as well as technical skills in building and real estate markets and management. However, many of the citizens and local stakeholders such as small businesses were not prepared to understand complex planning procedures. It proved necessary to invest both in developing the communication skills of the professionals and in training citizens in planning and civic participation.

Nevertheless Hoogvleit is notable for the scale of the project, its vision and strategic nature. It has focused on many different actions, but all of them were strategically aligned to tackle the deep rooted problems of social exclusion that had blighted the satellite town. It is an example of a community-driven regeneration process where there is also strong support from different tiers of government and from the semi-private housing corporations. There were strong and effective leadership and partnerships that worked.

5.2 Strategy and vision

Strategic plans have enjoyed varied success in terms of community acceptance and implementation. Critiques have focused on the fact that strategic plans tend to be top-down, give little consideration to the diagnostic tools that are used, are expensive, lack inclusiveness and are often ignored after being adopted.

Skills development needs to address these deficiencies because strategic plans remain an important means of expressing a public vision for a place. Lessons can be learned from situations, again from a very different context, where the need for strategic action was recognized, but barriers and skills gaps were important. An approach to this is illustrated in the following case study from Kenya.

Case Study 14: KENYA

Participation for neighbourhood plans in Kitale

In Kenya, the Local Authority Service Delivery Action Plans (LASDAP) programme aimed to get the community engaged in identifying their priorities for investment in service improvement. Plans created in this process were meant to determine the allocation of funds and identification of strategies. However, in many cases, the programme did not go low enough. It stopped at the electoral ward level, where it tended to get hijacked. In other cases, community consultation and collaboration easily became politically driven and lost transparency. Local authorities often involved representatives of only a few powerful community organizations and the large number of the poor lost out.

© Mansoor Ali

Source:
Mansoor Ali

Contact:
Mansoor Ali
International Urban
Programme Manager
Practical Action (ITDG)
Bourton on Dunsmore
Rugby CV23 9QZ, UK
e-mail: mansali@practi-calaction.org.uk

In response to shortcomings in implementing LASDAP at a local level, Practical Action, a UK-based charity, formed a partnership with Kitale Municipal Council, community groups and NGOs to ensure that the consultation process included low-income and informal communities.

In 2001, a systematic scan survey was conducted to identify and map needs for a wide range of services across all 10 wards of Kitale. An inventory of all stakeholders was developed to identify potential partners and areas of collaboration. The survey identified the informal settlements in greatest need and three were prioritized. A participatory neighbourhood planning approach in each settlement produced development and investment plans and guided the formulation of innovative solutions to sanitation, transportation and other issues. Furthermore, collaboration provided key changes to help efforts towards:

☐ understanding needs and priorities of the urban poor;

☐ mainstreaming the voices of the urban poor through better communication;

☐ developing sustainable partnerships, leading to resolution of issues such as land tenure;

☐ partnering with organizations of the poor and NGOs working in the area;

☐ assisting communities in mobilization, supporting local management and collective organizations;

☐ developing specific neighbourhood plans and linking them to ward- and city-level planning processes;

☐ influencing the allocation of financial resources in favour of community priorities.

> Efforts in Kitale have provided an opportunity to use similar approaches elsewhere and have gradually removed the barriers that restrict the use of such approaches. The project developed and tested a number of generic approaches to conduct neighbourhood-based planning with the involvement of community groups. Experience has been gained on developing effective partnerships and linking neighbourhood planning to the ward and town levels.

One of the key lessons from the Kitale experience was that Practical Action was able to respond in an imaginative and catalytic way that restructured, but took forward, the strategic planning process. The plans they have developed in cooperation have resulted in affected communities playing a larger role in infrastructure and service planning, thereby strengthening their capacity to learn and act to improve conditions in future efforts. The use of techniques such as scan surveys, stakeholder inventories and other participatory methods again emphasizes the importance of the skills of communication, negotiation and mediation discussed in Chapter 4. While professional training and administrative structures can compartmentalize thinking, working with low-income communities focuses attention on the need to think and act in an integrated manner and to develop and share generic skills.

5.3 Leadership skills and selling the vision

Leadership matters. A good leader is apt at finding opportunities and bringing others into the process of exploring these opportunities. In selling vision and action, a leader does not push or pull people into motion, but rather, he or she leads from the middle, promoting ideas through positive example. Leadership skills involve an awareness of how strategic ideas are generated through dialogue and discussion. Above all, effective leaders have a capacity for understanding the perceptions and aspirations of their constituents and responding to them by building consensus and fostering widely acceptable objectives.

Leaders exist at all levels and in all sectors. It is important, for strategic purposes, to strengthen alliances between leaders and combine their capacity to understand, analyze and mobilize in specific contexts.

Leadership can be especially crucial if there is hostility to the vision, as will often be the case. Case Study 15 shows how leadership can work in practice, even in the face of long-established prejudices.

Case Study 15: BULGARIA

Leadership and vision for the scaling-up of Romani school desegregation

Roma people and communities in Central and Eastern Europe face widespread discrimination, segregation and hostility. In Bulgaria, like many other countries in the region, these sentiments have persistently been reflected, among other ways, in public education. The overwhelming majority of Romani children attend segregated schools. In order to address this long-standing problem, Drom, a Roma-led organisation, teamed with the Open Society Institute Budapest's Roma Participation Programme (RPP) to develop a high-impact civic desegregation campaign led by Romani NGOs.

The work began in 2000. Strong local and international leadership was a feature. The project undertook to develop a model of good practice at the local level in Vidin in order to show that integration could work. Building up to this stage there were intensive preparatory steps taken to develop a vision for desegregation. These included round table discussions involving education directors, school teaching staff, Roma and non-Roma community representatives, public debates and extensive media coverage to render the process completely transparent. This was necessary to cultivate the necessary consensus for successful integration and to ensure that the receiving schools would provide a welcoming environment. The partnerships formed in these stages between Romani parents, the staff and directors of the mainstream schools consolidated and legitimated the process.

In subsequent stages, the project's leadership began to advocate for the replication of the Vidin model and to build national and international coalitions of support to advocate for substantive governmental reform to address the issue of segregation. Desegregation campaigns were Romani-led and committed to empowering Romani parents to make informed choices about their children's futures. The campaigns very publicly and practically countered the pervasive prejudice that Roma do not value education.

Continuing after the first pilot project in Vidin, RPP-funded projects were extended to more than 2,500 children in eight cities across Bulgaria, with participants showing marked improvements over children remaining in segregated education. In 2001, Petar Stoyanov, then the President of the Republic of Bulgaria, fully endorsed the Vidin initiative and expressed the hope that very soon 'the experience of Vidin will be common practice in the rest of Bulgaria'.

Even more striking than the rapid scaling-up and success of the Vidin model was the community effort to provide social support. Social workers visited every Romani family that had school-age children. Tutors were available for children who needed help. Teachers received special training. Families that needed food or clothing received assistance. Roma and non-Roma children shared outings, social events and cultural experiences.

Leadership and vision were crucial in the Vidin initiative. Rumyan Russinov and Donka Panajotova were key to this. Long before desegregation was on anybody's agenda concerning Roma, Russinov, the director of the RPP between 2000 and 2005, began campaigning. His leadership was instrumental in bringing together the non-governmental coalition of Roma and pro-Roma organizations that succeeded in bringing the Bulgarian government to the table and adopting the Framework Program for Equal Opportunities in April 1999.

Source:
Bernard Rorke

Contacts:
Bernard Rorke
Director
Roma Participation
Programme
Open Society Institute
H-1051 Budapest
Hungary
Tel: +361 327 3858 e-mail:
brorke@osi.hu

Rumyan Russinov
Deputy Director
Roma Education Fund
H-1056 Budapest
Váci.u 63
Hungary
Tel: +361 235-8030
e-mail: info@romaeduca-
tionfund.org

Donka Panajotova
Director
NGO 'Organization Drom'
Vidin 3700
k/s 'Saedinenie', bl.4, parter
Bulgaria
Tel: +359 94 606 209
e-mail:
organization_drom@lycos.c
om

© Organisation 'Drom' - Vidin

Commitments from the Bulgarian government provided opportunities for civil society initiatives and Romani-led advocacy. Russinov's persistent efforts succeeded in firmly establishing school desegregation on the public agenda, and led the way in internationalising the issue. Importantly, at national level, he had the legitimacy and credibility to hold together a coalition of Romani NGOs, educational experts and human rights activists. Russinov also had the negotiating skills to engage other stakeholders and bring local and national governments into dialogue.

At the local level, Panajotova, the leader of Drom and a former teacher, used her proven record in education, her charisma and her management and motivational skills to form a team sharing her passion for developing this project. Her context-specific expertize and contacts within the educational system, combined with her NGO experience as well as her intelligence, imagination and generosity of spirit were central to mobilizing willing partners and popularizing the idea of school desegregation among sceptical Romani and non-Romani community members.

This is an example of strategic leadership. One of the key skills it illustrates is inclusive visioning. The vision of desegregation had to be developed, advocated, explained, repeated and defended. Part of the skill of leadership is to be a champion and advocate, while at the same time empowering others. It helps to be charismatic, but charisma depends on legitimacy, credibility and the possession of motivational skills. These factors in turn depend on the ability to connect with others, to find ways to articulate their own hopes and aspirations, but also to listen to them and learn from them. Visions also require confidence, ambition, opportunism and risk taking, but always the leader has to be rooted in realities and aware of constraints.

5.4 Summary

Strategic action is essential if settlements are to be made more sustainable. Disjointed efforts, with different levels of government and different agencies at any one level pulling in opposite directions are recipes for failure. They waste scarce resources. However, these conditions are more the norm than the exception. In many countries the tradition has been that schools close their doors to the community when the children leave home; that health professionals focus on remedying illness rather than educating people in how to prevent illness; police chase those who commit crime, but rarely make links with the rest of the community and so on. Each profession and government department have tended to see just one dimension, rarely the whole picture. Generic skills of inclusive visioning, advocacy and joined-up thinking have been weak.

To succeed, strategic planning and action cannot be a one-way top-down process. The more the strategic process engages with the urban poor, the more those experts involved in it will learn the skills of thinking in a holistic and integrated way.

Key lessons

- Skills are needed to ensure that strategic actions embody insights from communities and stakeholders who are essential to the implementation of those actions.

- Horizontal and vertical integration will sustain a vision and make it realistic; lack of support, conflicting priorities and inconsistencies between policies over time and/or space will undermine strategies.

- Leadership matters and leadership skills are important in developing and sharing a vision.

6 Management

Planning is a part of management, and management is part of planning. Therefore those involved in planning – both professionals and non-professionals – need management skills.

Over the last decade there have been concerted attempts to reform public administration in general. This movement, often referred to as New Public Management, is controversial since it typically advocates market testing, contracting out and privatization of public services, full cost recovery (which may exclude the poor), internal competition mechanisms and more. However, enhancement of management skills for planning does not require endorsement of this agenda. For example, 'marketization' and internal competition often fragment service delivery, and so set up structures that hinder integration and an understanding of the whole, and so are likely to work against sustainable development. Other aspects that have figured strongly in public service reform are consistent with the revamped understanding of planning that is being advocating here. Decentralization, citizen involvement, partnerships with NGOs and strategic planning and visioning are examples.

This chapter seeks to expose some of the management skills and challenges that are part and parcel of planning for sustainable development under conditions where the urbanization of poverty has to be addressed. Management is about being accountable for the use of resources – time, property, people, but also budgets. Therefore the chapter begins by looking at ways in which management of budgets can become accountable to the urban poor. Then partnerships and the skills of partnerships and team working are introduced. A radical shift is required to put sustainable development and poverty alleviation at the heart of planning in many countries. Section 6.3 asks what skills are involved in managing such change? It is followed by a discussion of how to mainstream these agendas.

6.1 Managing and accounting for budgets

Budgeting and resource allocation are fundamental to the implementation of plans and policies. So is accountability and transparency. However, these can often be rather private processes, buried in the dry statistics of balance sheets that are perused by the few.

Involving different actors in the management of resources is an effective way of ensuring that their voice is acknowledged and taken into account throughout the implementation of the development policies and plans. Initiatives managed and administrated at local level, in which the local communities have a say in what gets funded and by whom, are likely to be responsive to local needs. In fact, in most cities in low- and middle-income nations, a significant proportion of all homes and neighbourhoods, and the infrastructure and services they contain, are organized, built and managed by low-income groups and their community organizations. However, appropriate funding mechanisms and skills to support this are often lacking.

Some of the best known examples of increasing local government accountability are in Brazil. The practice of participatory budgeting was first developed in Puerto Alegre, which allowed citizen assemblies in each district to decide priorities for use of part of the city's revenues. Participatory budgeting allows formerly excluded groups to participate in deciding on investment priorities in their communities and to monitor government responsiveness. Experience in many Brazilian cities has shown that such approaches result in more effective pro-poor expenditures and greater local government accountability.

Setting up locally-managed funds or local institutions through which national or local governments, international agencies and/or private actors can channel resources directly can also be an effective way of supporting local initiatives. It shifts the decision-making process and most of the administrative and transaction costs to where the initiatives are being managed. From there, it is much easier, quicker and cheaper to check on proposals and monitor their implementation using a network of people with local knowledge in the location.

Managing and administrating funds locally also means improved flexibility and promptness in response to the changes happening on the ground. It allows for more accountability to the intended beneficiaries at local level. These, in turn, are enticed to contribute their own resources to the initiative and ensure that user fees and taxes are collected. Indeed, many approaches involving the active participation of organized communities and civil society groups have demonstrated real effectiveness in the mobilization of resources outside the formal planning system. Case Study 16 shows how devolved budgeting can work to reduce poverty.

Case Study 16: INDIA

Bridging the finance gap at the local level for effective community-led solutions in urban development

Photo:
Community Toilet/bath house block, Mumbai

© Patrick Wakely

The Community-Led Infrastructure Finance Facility (CLIFF) began as a pilot project in 2002. It is a donor-funded scheme aimed at providing direct support to representative organizations of the urban poor to help them carry out community-driven initiatives in infrastructure, housing and urban services at city level in conjunction with municipalities and the private sector.

Organizations of the urban poor are developing the capacity to manage slum upgrading, resettlement and infrastructure initiatives. However, there is a chronic lack of medium-term credit available to allow them to launch larger scale projects. Commercial banks dislike lending to organizations that have no form of conventional collateral. Like most city officials, local politicians and developers, they lack confidence in the success of community-led processes.

Further information:
Homeless International web pages on CLIFF offer a wide range of information on CLIFF experiences in India and Kenya. CLIFF monitoring reports and annual reviews, background research documents from Homeless International's Bridging the Finance Gap in Housing and Infrastructure project, as well as several documents and articles about CLIFF are also downloadable from the Homeless International website:
http://www.homeless-international/cliff

D'Cruz, C. and Satterthwaite, D. (2005) Building Homes, Changing Official Approaches: The Work of Urban Poor Organisations and their Federations and their Contributions to Meeting the Millennium Development Goals in Urban Areas, IIED Working Paper on Poverty Reduction in Urban Areas no. 16, IIED, London. This article can be downloaded from IIED website:
http://www.iied.org/pubs/pdf/full/9547IIED.pdf

Burra, S. (2005) 'Towards a pro-poor framework for slum upgrading in Mumbai, India', Environment and Urbanisation, 17 (1) pp67–88.

SPARC website
http://www.sparcindia.org
and Nirman website
http://www.nirman.org

CLIFF channels official bilateral aid directly to organizations of slum and pavement dwellers, who can draw and manage a large capital fund and use it for a set of projects, which they can develop, implement and manage.

The funds are administered by the Cities Alliance Group on behalf of the two main donors: the UK's Department for International Development (DFID) and the Swedish International Development Cooperation Agency (Sida). The UK NGO Homeless International coordinates CLIFF at the international level and contributes finance from its 'guarantee fund'.

At local level, CLIFF funds are managed by the Indian Alliance, which is composed of four large organizations: the National Slum Dwellers Federation (NSDF), a growing network of around 650,000 poor families spanning over 70 cities; Mahila Milan, a network of women's savings collectives; the support NGO SPARC, and Nirman, a non-profit organization created to be the official implementing agency of CLIFF at the local level in India. CLIFF provides the Alliance with different forms of financial assistance. In particular, it sets a financial mechanism to make a large capital available to the Alliance in the forms of bridging loans on their demand.

The scaling-up process of local community-driven initiatives begins when projects are selected by the NSDF from a pool of initiatives undertaken by local organizations and federations of the urban poor on the basis of a number of criteria agreed upon by the Indian Alliance, Homeless International and technical advisory groups. Once projects are approved, CLIFF provides some capital bridging loans to kick start initiatives while negotiations with formal finance institutions and public officials begin. These projects are selected and implemented as 'flagships' to provide precedent for future scaling-up and pro-poor policy change.

By June 2005, CLIFF capital funds had supported 13 community-led development projects in India, many of which had been initiated by the Alliance in the past, but which were hindered by financial problems. Ten of the projects are based around housing and three around sanitation. These projects enable the Alliance to strategically engage with government and challenge 'business as usual' in terms of planning, municipal procurement and building regulation, so that they better benefit the urban poor. More importantly, the projects allow the Alliance to develop new working partnerships with both government and private sector institutions, in which the resources that different groups bring to the solution are recognized and respected. This is done through the demonstration of effective approaches and practices, which can then be replicated on a larger scale ranging from settlement to city and even national levels.

Because the goal of CLIFF is to produce locally viable solutions that yield scaleable, affordable and deliverable housing and infrastructure to the urban poor, one of the scheme's objectives is to help the Alliance leverage money from other external sources and spread financial stakes. Projects are planned on the basis of a project revenue stream, allowing loan finance to be repaid. For example, projects can be used to initiate the release of subsidies or contracted payments from local, state and central government. Additional revenue can also be drawn in from sales of residential units, commercial space or plots.

CLIFF's loan finances and support grants ensure that communities can begin work on a project and develop it to a certain stage before they can secure project revenues from government or other sources. This initial capital is also meant to help the Alliance cope with delays in funding disbursements and late-payments by their government partners (the Alliance refuses to pay any bribes!). In some cases it has helped to leverage land and infrastructure provision directly from local authorities. By June 2005, allocated CLIFF capital funds of just over GB£5 million were projected to draw in revenues totalling over GB£25 million for the portfolio of 13 projects.

The Alliance has also managed to negotiate loan finance from formal financial institutions and to use CLIFF to negotiate pre-financing with private contractors, who are required to invest their own funds and share some of the risk associated with the project.

The CLIFF process also works most effectively where local authorities are open to new approaches and willing to work collaboratively with organizations of the urban poor. It also works best where financial markets are sufficiently developed to enable banks and other financial institutions to begin a process of dialogue on provision of financial services to the urban poor.

Source:
Malcolm Jack (Homeless International UK)

Contacts:
Homeless International
Queens House
16 Queens Road
Coventry CV1 3DF
United Kingdom
Tel: +44 (0) 24 76632802
Fax: +44 (0) 24 76632911
Website:
http://www.homeless-international.org

SPARC (the Society for the Promotion of Area Resource Centre)
PO Box 9389
Bhulabhai Desai Road
Mumbai 400 026
India
Tel: +91 22 2386 5053 / +91 22 2385 8785
Fax: +91 22 2388 7566
e-mail: admin@sparcindia.org / sparc@vsnl.in

This case study illustrates how financial management and budgeting skills can be used to benefit the urban poor. These skills are part of the capacity needed to develop creative and sustainable solutions in urban development. Such schemes enable the poor to address their needs and strengthen their position in relation to the other actors involved in urban development.

However, as the case study shows, these skills are complemented by others. Negotiation is again important. Another skill is the ability to scale-up a project that works so that it can be replicated and deliver wider benefits. Last but not least, there are skills of networking, team working and partnership.

6.2 Building and sustaining partnerships

New directions in public management increasingly emphasize the importance of partnerships with private enterprises and/or civil society and non-governmental actors for the development of urban infrastructure and services and the management of contracts. Partnerships are an effective means of surmounting the lack of funds and combining existing resources in urban development. By engaging different actors in the development process, partnerships have a higher potential to offer sustainable solutions that respond to the needs and interests of the different parties.

If planning is to be pro-poor then marginalized groups must have a place at the partnership table. This can be done, as Case Study 17 shows.

Case Study 17: BOLIVIA

Partnering for more efficient and affordable water supply

The Agua para Todos (Water for All) initiative in Cochabamba, Bolivia describes how a municipal water company, a private consortium, local communities and a non-profit foundation, with support from the municipal authorities and the United Nations Development Programme (UNDP), have joined into an entrepreneurial partnership to extend residents' access to affordable water.

Locally-managed water supply systems are common in Bolivia, especially in rural and peri-urban areas. 54 per cent of water supply systems in the country are managed by committees, 25 per cent by cooperatives, 11 per cent by municipalities and the rest by other organizations, including private companies. Despite being acknowledged by national policies of decentralization and local government, locally-managed water supply systems do not fit neatly into national policies and plans for water and sanitation, especially at the peri-urban level.

In the suburban areas of Cochabamba, the municipal water company, SEMAPA, lacked the finance to build secondary water distribution networks, leaving hundreds of homes without a connection to the main water supply. In response, local communities organized themselves into water committees to initiate their own water provision systems. The Agua Tuya (Your Water) Programme, initiated by Plastioforte, a private manufacturing and distribution consortium, served the water committees but worked autonomously from the public water company. Despite the amount of activity in Cochabamba, attempts to improve water supply remained uncoordinated and inefficient and faced the risk of future stresses due to population growth.

The Agua para Todos initiative attempted to join actors in an innovative partnership model. The main idea was to overcome the lack of coordination and improve efficiency and to combine partners' resources to avoid the prohibitive costs of establishing new secondary water connections and reduce the cost of water for consumers. Within the Agua para Todos partnership, Agua Tuya constructed secondary water systems on behalf of the water committees while coordinating with SEMAPA, which planned where to direct its main water pipelines. The NGOs CIDRE and Pro Habitat Foundation provide a loan to each water committee to finance the cost of construction. Each system is meant to serve from 100–500 households with a single main water entry point. SEMAPA can connect its network to these points and sell water in bulk by contracting directly with the water committee rather than each household individually. This contributes to reducing the final cost of water for the users by creating aggregated demand.

In a year since March 2005, seven systems have been completed, benefiting over 5,000 people and cutting the unit cost of water by half. Indeed, once the municipal water supply connects this sub-network to its main pipeline, the cost will be further reduced to just one tenth of the original price per cubic meter. Future plans for the project aim to provide 17,000 connections serving 85,000 people within the next five years.

Important skills that underpinned the partnership's success were the coordination efforts from each partner organization and the willingness to make the most of the partnership synergies. Coordination was mostly bilateral as partners would approach each other separately on a needs basis. Although this approach worked reasonably well, it may become increasingly inefficient and time-consuming as the scale of the project increases. In addition, more institutionalized mechanisms will be needed to sustain a good level of communication and cooperation between partners.

Despite a lack of formal structures, a high degree of transparency was key to sustaining the partnership and keeping

© Agua Tuya

the different organizations motivated and receptive to solving project-related challenges together. Agua Tuya was seen as playing a lead role in this regard, for example, by setting up and moderating an on-line group where members could read and make comments about progress and/or any issues. The website and the drafting of the new activity plan left ample scope for discussion, preparation and then feedback and modification.

© Agua Tuya

Source:
Gustavo Heredia

Contact:
Gustavo Heredia
DirectorPrograma Agua Tuya
Casilla 6264
Cochabamba
Bolivia
Tel: +591 4 424 5193
Fax: +591 4 411 6592
Mob: +591 707 10321

Website:
http://aguatuya.com

e-mail:
gustavoh@aguatuya.com
gustavoh@grupoforte.net

The active participation of the communities in the decision making, financing, implementation and administration of services generated strong local ownership. In all the systems, infrastructure was built with the participation of users, who, in most cases, contributed with labour and finances. This explains why residents consider themselves 'right holders' rather than users of their water systems, and feel entitled to make decisions about the management of their water provision. Moreover, the involvement of civil society in the project acted as a strong socio-political stabilizer in an area usually characterized by disorder and lack of coordination.

The partners' involvement in the partnership was also supported by training and capacity building activities. Both Agua Tuya/Plastioforte and Pro Habitat provided back-up support and guidance to community-management structures regarding the operation and administration of their systems. At least one person from every community was provided with on-the-job training as a plumber for system operation and maintenance during the construction process. This practical training during installation was then complemented by one month of training at the Plastioforte factory resulting in certification as a qualified plumber. Once the system is completed, the water committee is given some follow-up training and support.

The Agua para Todos initiative shows the main ingredients in the development of a successful management partnership. The stakeholders' willingness and commitment to work together towards shared objectives is crucial. Communication and transparency between the partners promote the sustainability of the partnership. It is also notable that training and skills development has been built into the project.

Skills in brokerage, coordination and project management are evident in this innovative partnership-based project. Evaluation skills are also used to quantify the effectiveness of the project by measuring the extent and quality of the water service being delivered. Not least important among the outcomes is the significant cost reductions achieved. Such savings make water more affordable and so help the poor, and are measures of efficiency gains. The ability to monitor and measure efficiency in an appropriate way is important in any use of resources.

6.3 Change management

Initiating processes that will lead to sustainable changes remains one of the main challenges. Scaling-up is more than a quantitative process; it invariably entails a change in the quality of the solutions provided and the practices by which they are implemented. Tackling urban poverty is a multi-sectoral task that requires continuous cooperation and coordination among the range of actors involved at various levels.

At project level, action is needed to upgrade the built environment and improve the material living conditions of the poor alongside initiatives for social development (educational, cultural, health or leisure-related) to address the causes and consequences of poverty with a long-term perspective.

At policy level, coordination between sectors involves joint decision making and the co-development of policy and plans and the collaborative management of programmes. This can include different sectors of government authorities at central and city level, private stakeholders and civil society, with special representation of the communities directly affected by the plans. High levels of cooperation require an institutional framework and mechanisms to allow all groups to participate and take action together that allows initiatives to effectively trigger processes of change beyond the project level.

Case Study 18 highlights the importance of continuous cooperation and inclusion throughout the implementation process, directly involving communities and their organizations in the management of the initiatives that affect them, thereby benefiting from their skills and resources in an effective way.

Case Study 18: BRAZIL

Initiating inclusive processes at city scale

Rio de Janeiro is characterized by divisions between the formal city and the favelas. The divisions affect every part of life, from access to health, education, transport and safety, to secure employment and influence over resource allocation and policy. Favela Bairro ('slum-to-neighbourhood') was a city-scale slum upgrading programme launched in 1994 by the Housing Department of the Municipal Government of Rio (SMH) with the support of the Inter-American Development Bank (IDB) to tackle the physical and social integration of Rio's squatter settlements into the formal city. Through the implementation of upgrading projects in each of Rio's medium-sized favelas, the objective was not only to improve living conditions for the urban poor, but to initiate a longer term process of integration on a city-scale, turning favelas into Rio neighbourhoods and their residents into citizens of Rio.

Favela Bairro tackled this issue through an integrated approach that attempted to provide favelas with access to services and infrastructure similar to those available in the rest of the city. The physical upgrading aimed to complement or construct basic urban infrastructure through the instal-

Source:
Jorge Fiori

Contact:
Jorge Fiori
Development Planning Unit (DPU)
University College London (UCL)
Website:
http://www.ucl.ac.uk/dpu
e-mail: j.fiori@ucl.ac.uk

lation of basic sanitation and circulation systems, allowing for the free movement of people and vehicles (where possible), and better access to public services. At the same time, the programme introduced urban symbols of the formal city, such as roads, squares, infrastructure and a menu of social services from daycare centres, adult education, job training to advice for securing land tenure to support social inclusion in the favelas. The underlying idea was that the 'opening up' of favelas to the outside world, and the creation of new public spaces, would transform the relationship between government and the local community, and trigger change at city-scale. In this way, urban integration was promoted as an instrument for comprehensive social inclusion.

A key to Favela Bairro's success in meeting different causes and manifestations of urban poverty was its multi-sectoral character, and its implementation on a scale large enough to include the city as a whole.

At the project level, the programme aimed to impact on different aspects of urban poverty by allying infrastructure upgrading with social development initiatives, though in practice, the latter was often disregarded at the expense of the former. Each settlement project involved a large variety of different actors, ranging from architects and private construction firms to NGOs and many municipal government departments. Beneficiaries were also invited to participate throughout the project, though sometimes to a limited extent.

At the policy level, Favela Bairro involved more municipal departments and public sector bodies than any non-conventional housing programme previously implemented in Rio. The SMH quickly had to develop the skills to liaise, contract out and negotiate with a large number of actors. This was done with varying levels of success, as the skills needed to manage contracts with construction firms differ greatly from those needed to deal with architects, community groups and hostile drug traffickers.

The SMH was not fully prepared to promote and accept participation. It failed to delegate decision making powers to some actors, especially community organizations and NGOs representing the interests of the favela communities. The participation of favela residents was set within a top-down structure defined by the SMH. There were no mechanisms in place to systematically identify who the most vulnerable residents were within particular settlements and assess their specific needs. Moreover, a greater range of needs and problems could have been more effectively addressed if some municipal and state actors had been involved more fully. Control over the programme mostly remained in the hands of the SMH.

The lack of institutional mechanisms guaranteeing multi-sectoral cooperation between the different actors, including the necessary mechanism to secure the active involvement of the favela communities, was probably one of the major factors to undermine the continuity of Favela

© Alberto Lopez

Further information:
Brakarz, J., Greene, M. and Rojas, E. (2002) Cities for All: Recent Experiences with Neighborhood Upgrading Programs, Inter-American Development Bank, Washington DC.
Fiori, J., Ramirez, R. and Riley, E. (2000) Urban Poverty Alleviation Through Environmental Upgrading in Rio de Janeiro: Favela Bairro, DPU Research Report R7343, Development Planning Unit, London.
Fiori, J., Riley, E. and Ramirez, R. (2004) 'Melhoria física e integração social no Rio de Janeiro: O caso do Favela Bairro, Brasil Urbano, MAUAD, Rio de Janeiro.

Websites:
IDB website with links to reports on Favela Bairro:
http://www.idb.org

Rio de Janeiro municipal government website on the Favela Bairro programme:
http://www.fau.ufrj.br/prou rb/cidades/favela/frames.ht ml

Housing Department of Rio's municipal government website on the Favela Bairro programme:

http://www.rio.rj.gov.br/hab itacao/

Photo:
Favela Bairro, Andarai, Rio de Janeiro

Bairro itself, as it was not able to resist the political fluctuations and changes of mood in public opinion over time. The programme slowed down by the newly elected Mayor in 2000. Since the latest municipal elections in 2004, it appears that it has gained in increased attention and political commitment again, yet in a very different context where most of the support from the public and the administration has been lost. Rising levels of violence associated with drug trafficking have negatively impacted on public opinion towards favelas. Their residents remain segregated from Rio's formal life and political arena.

Through both its success and failures, the Favela Bairro experience shows that appropriate and institutionalized delegation of decision making and managing powers is essential in order to impact beyond settlement level to that of the city, with the potential to trigger true processes of social inclusion, in a sustainable manner. Horizontally, multi-sectoral coordination between the actors is needed, but there also need for vertical connections, down to civil society level.

In short, the ambitious vision in the Favela Bairro programme floundered. Coordination is easier to prescribe than to deliver. Teamworking is unlikely to be effecvtive if there are significant institutional gaps and wavering political commitment. Achieving 'joined-up thinking' among people from different backgrounds and with different agendas in various sectors – public, private, NGO, community and academic – is normally difficult. Without coherent collaboration, the implementation of multi-objective urban renewal is difficult, if possible at all and substantial funds can be sunk into compartmentalized initiatives without producing the desired and lasting results. Case Study 19 describes another attempt to design and deliver an integrated planning process.

Case Study 19: NIGERIA

Dynamic Planning for an integrated development strategy in the Niger Delta

The concept of Dynamic Planning was developed by a planning consultancy and applied in the Niger Delta region of Nigeria. The name reflects the focus on dynamic processes of change, brought on by the dynamic relationships between stakeholders and planners that are explored during consultative workshops, and the dynamic plans for management of change, which encompass delivery and are capable of adaptation to new phenomena. Various tools and techniques have been adapted from 'game theory' and other interactive techniques that have developed out of participatory scenario-writing and 'rational choice theory' for each stage of the plan-making process.

The process starts with 'consultation', which is focused and structured. Selected participants who represent the main actors in the public, private, NGO and community sectors are asked first to define the 'problems' (who is affected, who benefits and so on), then jointly draw diagrams of ongoing processes with their inter-related 'roots' of the problems. This exercise, managed by a planner, has proved very productive, building new knowledge and mutual understanding among members of the group. It produces ideas for a wide range of potential interventions.

Reducing smoke
The killer in the kitchen

Friday 23rd June, 8.30-10.30am
Room MR14
Vancouver Convention & Exhibition Centre

PRACTICAL ACTION
Technology challenging poverty

Reducing smoke
The killer in the kitchen

Smoke in the home from cooking fires leads to more than one and a half million premature deaths each year – and it is a problem that particularly affects the poor living on the fringes of cities in informal settlements.

Join us for a lively, interactive debate to explore whether international funding should be used to subsidise the price of technologies to tackle indoor smoke.

"This house believes that direct subsidies for improved technologies to reduce the 1.5 million deaths caused by indoor air pollution are always misguided."

- Chair – Professor Michael Brauer, The University of British Colombia
- Speaking for the motion – Keith Openshaw, Energy Consultant
- Speaking against – Don O'Neal, HELPS International

Case studies from Sudan and Nepal will be presented and the audience will have an opportunity to question the panel and cast their votes.

For more information visit Practical Action / ITDG Publishing stand 1217 in the WUF Exhibition.

www.practicalaction.org/smoke

Friday 23rd June, 8.30-10.30am
Room MR14
Vancouver Convention & Exhibition Centre

PRACTICAL ACTION
Technology challenging poverty

This is followed by the exploration of potential strategies for change, rather than just a compilation of proposed interventions. Integrating various interventions into a coherent strategy is done with an eye on a process of change: how the resources available can be used to influence future activities and trends, bearing in mind the linkages between activities. For example, what actions would have to be taken by an education authority, public transport providers, the police, land use planners and perhaps house builders in order to influence a certain socio-economic group to return to live in a town centre?

Selecting between alternative strategies or interventions is also related to the core concept of process and stakeholders. The options have to be assessed in terms of their feasibility and their impacts. Feasibility, namely the likelihood of the process of future change materializing, can be put to the test in discussion with 'active stakeholders' of all sectors whose decisions and actions will affect the change. Impacts are the way the changes throughout the process will be experienced by recipient stakeholders. Impacts will be created as repercussions from each step of implementation, not only from the 'final outcome'. Putting their heads together, both active and recipient stakeholders can contribute to drawing the total picture of likely impacts. The approach should reveal not only the achievement of desired objectives, but also predictable side effects that may be beneficial or detrimental, thereby contributing to the sustainability of the planning and development process as a continuum.

Source:
Dalia Lichfield

Contact:
Dalia Lichfield
Lichfield Planning
51 Chalton Street
London NW1 1HY
e-mail: d.lichfield@lichfield-planning.co.uk
Website: www.lichfield-planning.co.uk

Integrated planning as 'management of change' requires several anticipatory or 'scenario constructing' skills and techniques. Key among them is the ability to see the environment as a multi-dimensional set of interactions, where different stakeholders have different outlooks and rules and to know how to address all without marginalizing any, unless they are universally socially unacceptable – a tall order!

Change management also requires capacity building. Electing municipal government for the first time is a change by any standards. However, Case Study 20 shows that Mozambique soon realized that for decentralization to succeed there was a need for new institutional structures at the community level to promote dialogue between government and civil society.

Case Study 20: MOZAMBIQUE

Improving municipal governance in Dondo

In 1998, the first municipal elections were held in Mozambique based on a new legal framework for decentralization. Dondo, in Sofala province, was one of 33 municipalities that chose their city council and its president. Despite the government's intention to involve citizens in municipal development, the institutional framework and mechanisms for community participation and involvement in local development did not exist.

Already in 1996, NGOs in Dondo had expressed the need for an awareness raising and capacity building processes for civil society, since citizens lacked an understanding of their role in urban governance and development. The demand was integrated into the design of a project on civil society

Sources:
Hemma Tengler (member of the Dondo programme team)
Josef Pampalk (member of the Dondo programme team)

© Dondo Programme Team

Photo:
Prioritising local problems

Further information:
Roque, C. and Tengler, H. (2000) Dondo no Dhondo, Desenvolvimento Municipal Participativo, Beira.
Pampalk, J. (2003) Nzerumbawiri. Proverbios Sena: Dinamizar o Densenvolvimento Comunitário Valorizando a Literatura Oral, Maputo
The experience of Dondo in civil society participation in municipal governance is listed among the UN-Habitat's best practices in urban governance and presented on the Best Practices website at:
http://www.bestpractices.org/database/

Contacts:
Gimo de Carmo Lourenço
ASVIMO (local NGO partner in the implementation of community development projects)
Centro de Viúvas e Orfaos

no Bairro de Mafarinha
Dondo, Mozambique
Tel: +258-82-5502800

participation in municipal governance, for which funding was successfully negotiated with the Austrian Cooperation agency. The project was a pioneer initiative in the country at the time and took place in a legal and political context in which community participation in decision making had not yet been institutionalized and was only accepted reluctantly. It had the purpose of making municipal governance sustainable through actively involving local communities and their stakeholders in the planning and implementation of development measures. This could not have been achieved without the persistent work of the centro de serviço in the region, which was crucial to building people's capacity to mobilize and participate in the eight bairros (townships) of Dondo.

The first phase of the project began with a training programme for resident activists and a civic education campaign in Dondo's bairros. About a third of all households were visited and told about the role of citizens in local government. Information on the problems that affected them as well as data on local infrastructure was gathered, then incorporated into the bairros' profiles and presented at community meetings. It was during these meetings that participants in each bairro elected their representatives and marked the beginning of the township development committees (núcleos de desenvolvimento de bairro – NDBs).

The next step was for each bairro to elaborate a short-, medium- and long-term development plan based on the needs acknowledged in the survey and have it approved by the residents. An important skill transmitted during their elaboration was the capacity to think strategically and to prioritize. Bairro profiles and development plans were presented to the city council, which, at a three-day planning workshop in July 1999, agreed to incorporate the community plans into the municipal development plan.

In the second half of 1999, the development committees started tackling the implementation of different social infrastructure projects based on those plans. In each bairro, there was one project based on the use of local resources and one tapping onto external donor funding but with contributions from the community. This required activists and members of the development committees to mobilize and build motivation among bairro residents. A cycle of three education campaigns (on improving the urban environment, girls' education and public health) was carried out during 2000 with active community involvement. A third phase of the project started, when the council took ownership of the participatory planning process and invited the development committees and other stakeholders to set up a Municipal Development Committee that was to take an active part in the budgeting of activities for the following years.

The pioneer experience of Dondo's bairro development committees over the years had a positive impact on the development of local governance on a national scale, as citizen representation (at least consultative) has become mandatory in 120 districts and beyond the 33 municipalities in which the first city councils were elected. The creation and consolidation of a new institutional structure on a community level (similar to the NDBs on Dondo) and the promotion of dialogue between government and civil society brought about positive changes in the government's attitude towards community-based initiatives. Citizens' representatives are now included in a consultative process, the use and allocation of technical resources at the local level have become more respectful of communities' needs and priorities, and the overall coordination between the government and civil society has significantly improved. Through capacity-building activities, citizens' representatives are increasingly assuming their role to guarantee transparency in the allocation and use of resources at the local level.

People's attitudes have also changed, as they have learnt how to mobilize their potential and gained confidence, a better sense of ownership and an increased willingness to engage in improving their living environment – which was a crucial motor for the whole initiative. As a result, the quality of life and public health situation in Dondo have improved in a sustainable way.

The regional broadcasting programme of Radio Mozambique in Beira and the local community radios were also important. By spreading information and interacting with the population in their first language, they contributed much to improving participation and transparency in Dondo's municipal governance.

A key to the success of the initiative thus lies in linking the creation and training of civil society institutions while implementing concrete projects to improve living conditions in the bairros. One danger in Mozambique, however, the distinction made between capacity building for civil society and capacity building for governmental institutions, as it is more promising to coordinate them in a complementary process (such as in Case Study 7 on South African Integrated Development Plans). The future and sustainability of the municipal governance system in Mozambique will depend on efforts to persevere and continuously adapt and improve capacity building on both levels.

This case study shows the importance of change management, training skills and skills in using the media. However, didactic training in isolation is not likely to be effective. As the Dondo example shows, managing change involves planning and delivering training alongside the use of catalytic actions and projects that have visibility and demonstrate that real improvements in living conditions are happening. Devolving power and taking a pro-poor stance represent significant changes. Such changes need to be planned, supported by capacitybuilding – processes that need good management skills.

6.4 Institutionalization and mainstreaming

Institutionalization is the process by which changes are sustained in development. It means that practices become sufficiently regular and continuous that they amount to 'institutions'. That is to say that they are regularly and continuously repeated, and accepted as the proper way to do things. Good management is about being innovative and then ensuring that successful innovations in practice become 'institutions'. Part of the skill of management is to shift new but important concerns and practices from the edge of an organization into its 'core business'; from pilot project to regular practice.

The development of the Thai Community Organizations Development Institute (CODI) is a example of how different actors, communities, NGOs, local and national government authorities from different sectors, universities, and professionals from the private sector have learnt new skills

Contacts:

Members of the Dondo programme team:
c/o. Projecto DEC/CDS
Rua Major Serpa Pinto
Nº2000, 2ºandar
C.P. 69, Beira, Mozambique

Hemma Tengler
Tel: +258-82-6015670
e-mail:
hemmatengler@teledata.mz

Carlos Roque
Tel: +258-82-4072590
e-mail:
Carlosroquecr@yahoo.com.br

Josef Pampalk
Tel: +43-650-937 0427
e-mail:
josef.pampalk@gmx.at

Local Government and Civil Society actors involved in the Dondo initiative:

Manuel Cambezo
Presidente do Conselho Municipal do Dondo
Mozambique
Tel: +258-23-950409

José Louis Tesoura
Núcleo de Desenvolvimento da Cidade de Dondo and Núcleos de Desenvolvimento dos Bairros (representatives of the local communities)
Rua 25 de Setembro
Dondo, Mozambique.
Tel/Fax: +258-82-8001890

Paula Cristina de Oliveira Tavares Morreira
FUMASO (local NGO partner in the implementation of community development projects)
Centro Comunitário no Bairro Macharote
Dondo, Mozambique
Tel: +258-82-5650640

and worked out new processes on how to work together for city-wide development and urban poverty reduction. The case study shows how these skills and practices were gradually developed into institutionalized processes under the umbrella of a newly created government agency, CODI.

Case Study 21: THAILAND

Mainstreaming community-led processes for housing and urban poverty alleviation: The development of CODI and the Baan Mankong programme

Sources:
Somsook Boonayabanha
(CODI and ACHR)
Maurice Leonhardt and Tom
(ACHR)

Photo:
Household saving
management

© COD/ACHR

Contact:
Somsook Boonyabancha
Community Organizations
Development Institute
2044/31-32 Petchburitatmai
Road
Huaykhwang, Bangkok
10320
Thailand

Tel: +66 2 716 6000
Fax: +66 2 716 6001
e-mail: codi@codi.or.th

Launched by the Thai government in 2003 and implemented through the Community Organizations Development Institute, the Baan Mankong ('Secure Housing') programme has set itself the target of improving housing, living and tenure security for 300,000 households in 2000 poor communities in 200 Thai cities within five years. The programme operates differently from most conventional approaches in that government funds are channelled in the form of infrastructure subsidies and housing loans direct to poor communities' organizations and/or their networks, to allow them to plan and carry out improvements to their housing environment and basic services wherever possible, and to develop and work on city-wide upgrading programmes together with the city authorities, national agencies and other local actors.

The Urban Community Development Office (UCDO) was first set up by the government of Thailand in 1992 in order to address urban poverty. From the outset, UCDO sought to bring together different interest groups – with its board comprising senior government staff, academics and community representatives. This was critical to the recognition by UCDO that for pro-poor development to take place, relations between low-income groups and the state had to change.

Initially, loans were available to community-based savings and loan groups for income generation, revolving funds, housing and housing improvements. However, as the savings groups that worked with UCDO became more numerous and larger, it was decided to address scaling-up by providing loans to community networks that then on-lent to their member organizations. These city networks have particular importance for supporting city-wide upgrading programmes that are today part of the Baan Mankong programme.

By 2000, when UCDO's work was integrated into CODI (a government agency with its own legal entity, contrasting with UCDO placed within the National Housing Authority) 950 community savings groups had been established and supported in 53 out of Thailand's 75 provinces. Baan Mankong was specifically set up to support processes designed and managed by low-income households and their community organizations and networks. These community groups and networks work with local governments, professionals, universities and NGOs in their city to survey all poor communities and then plan an upgrading programme within three to four years. Once the plans have been finalized, CODI channels the infrastructure subsidies and housing loans directly to the communities.

Each upgrading programme builds on the community-managed programmes that CODI and its predecessor, UCDO, have supported since 1992 and on people's capacity to manage their needs collectively. They were made possible by what communities have already developed and how they have mobilized and joined together to form a network to work together and negotiate with city or provincial authorities, influence development planning or simply work together on shared problems of housing, livelihoods or access to basic services. For instance, in the city of Uttaradit, the initiative started with survey mapping of all the slums and small pockets of squatters, identifying landowners and those slums that could stay and that needed to be relocated. This helped link community organizations and began building a community network supported by young architects, a group of monks and the mayor. Together, they sought to find housing solutions for 1000 families within the existing city fabric through different techniques such as land sharing, reblocking, in situ upgrading and relocation. Their city-wide housing plan became the basis for the city upgrading programme under Baan Mankong and now includes infrastructure improvements, urban regeneration, canal cleaning, wasteland reclamation and park development.

Baan Mankong seeks to go to scale by supporting thousands of community-driven initiatives within city-wide programmes designed and managed by urban poor networks working in partnership with local actors. By September 2005, initiatives were underway in 415 urban poor communities involving more than 29,054 households. Where possible, relocation was avoided and most households received long-term land security – for instance through cooperative ownership or long-term leases to the community or to individual households.

The work of CODI stands is an example of how a government agency can actively support community-driven solutions for city-wide development and urban poverty reduction. The Baan Mankong initiative shows how different aspects of city management can be decentralized to communities – from public parks and markets, maintenance of drainage canals, solid waste collection and recycling to community welfare programmes. According to the director of CODI, 'opening up more room for people to become involved in the development of their city is the new frontier for urban management – and real decentralization', and 'Slum upgrading is a powerful way to spark off

© COD/ACHR

© COD/ACHR

Photo:
Charoenchai Nimitmai - before: community negotiation with their landowner to release land for their collective development

Charoenchai Nimitmai - after

Further information :
Community Development Fund, Experiences of UCDO/CODI, presented at UNCHS meeting in New York, available from the Shack Dwellers International website: http://www.sdinet.org/reports/r14.htm
Boonyabancha, S. (2003) A Decade of Change: From the Urban Community Development Office (UCDO) to the Community Development Institute (CODI) in Thailand, IIED Working Paper 12 on Poverty Reduction in Urban Areas, International Institute for Environment and Development, London
Boonyabancha, S. (2005) 'Baan Mankong: Going to scale with 'slum' and squatter upgrading in Thailand', Environment and Urbanization, 17 (1), pp21–46
CODI (2004) CODI Update 4, June, CODI, Bangkok, can also be downloaded from the ACHR website: http://www.achr.net/bann_mankong.htm

Further information:
CODI official website:
http://www.codi.or.th/ (in
Thai, with some pages
translated in English)
Asian Coalition for Housing
Rights web guide to Baan
Mankong:
http://www.achr.net/bmkgu
ide.htm (in English)

this kind of decentralisation'. Making development more favourable to low-income groups implies that these are involved in decision making, must be able to own the decisions that are taken, and must be in control of the activities that follow.

The Baan Mankong programme imposes as few conditions as possible in order to give urban poor communities, networks and stakeholders in each city the room to design their own programme. The challenge is to support upgrading in ways that allow urban poor communities to lead the process and generate local partnerships so that the whole city contributes to the solution.

Rather than ends in themselves, projects must be seen as part of a more comprehensive strategy driven by the poor to improve their living conditions and their relationship with the local institutions in charge of responding to some of their needs and priorities. Programmes such as Baan Mankong create space for people to think about the issues that affect them as a community, and provide tools and resources to translate their social development and community welfare ideas into facilities. In this way, 'Baan Mankong is helping to strengthen collective social processes, which improve security and well-being in many ways other than simply physical assets'.

So often time-limited projects fizzle out, teams scatter and momentum evaporates. Part of the skill of project management is to look beyond the end of the project, managing not just an exit strategy but driving the positive features and practices from the project into the mainstream, and creating new 'institutions'.

6.6 Summary

The management of urban development requires that decisions are implemented effectively and efficiently. A wide range of skills are involved, including preparing development plans, setting clear aims, drawing up and managing budgets, appraising projects, allocating responsibilities, entering partnerships, planning training and awarding and managing contracts. Good management requires flexibility to constantly adapt to an evolving context and the changing needs and priorities of citizens, clients and stakeholders while ensuring that the administration of urban service delivery is not disrupted.

Plans by themselves cannot deliver sustainable and pro-poor development. There has to be implementation and implementation needs management. In the long run, the administration of post-implementation processes matters more to consumers than the initial plans and development projects – ensuring that water runs through the pipes, roads are maintained, electricity is constantly supplied, sanitation and solid waste are healthily disposed of or recycled. The underpinnings of sustainable service delivery lie in routine preventive maintenance and public asset management. The skills required in the decision making, management and administration processes of an urban development initiative or policy are quite different. Yet it is important to emphasize the linkages between them because weakness in one undermine effectiveness in the other and impact on the whole of city development.

Key lessons

☐ Management skills matter. Planning needs to be efficient and effective.

☐ Management is not just a top-down process that is only the responsibility of senior officials or administrators.

☐ Management skills drive a sustainable and pro-poor planning agenda.

☐ Management skills are essential for successful implementation of plans and policies.

7 Monitoring and Learning

Planning must be responsive, flexible and therefore subject to constant monitoring, evaluation and reflection. This has been a recurring theme throughout this section. Planning is not a linear, start-to-finish processes. Planning is about innovation, about making a difference. Innovation comes out of the interplay of knowledge from inside and outside a company or organization, from sharing and adapting ideas through discussions with customers, users, stakeholders. It is about being willing to experiment and to learn.

Learning and the skills that making learning effective are therefore vitally important if progress is to be made in planning for more sustainable settlements. Some of that learning comes from having systems in place within an organization or project that prompt questions about whether aims are being achieved (or not achieved). Thus this chapter starts with discussion of monitoring and evaluation. We can also learn from and with others, which is the theme of section 7.2. Learning from practice is then discussed, before the chapter ends by stressing the need for reflective practitioners.

7.1 Monitoring and evaluation

Monitoring and evaluation are used by organizations as tools for judging results in terms of performance and specific achievements. The objectives of monitoring and evaluation processes are generally to enhance learning, improve decision making and hold actors accountable.

However, monitoring and evaluation are often misused or not used to deliver their potential. Monitoring and evaluation are inward looking and critical. However, these processes, like others in planning, must be opened to a wider group of actors. Information must be shared not hidden, left open to different interpretations and criticisms, not collected then buried. Monitoring and evaluation is usually more effective when it is handled by people who are to some extent engaged with context, rather than by outside, 'impartial' actors unfamiliar with the conditions before, during and after planned interventions.

The discussion and case studies that follow present some of the ways in which generic monitoring and learning can be incorporated into planning to ensure that they become part of the field's progressive future.

Case Study 22: PERU

The Cities for Life Forum and mainstreaming monitoring and evaluation

The area of Nuevo Chimbote, 420km north of Lima, was supposed to host the rapid urban growth coming from the city of Chimbote, which was largely destroyed by an earthquake in the early 1970s. To face this problem, government planning proposed to establish plots for self-constructed houses

© Cities for Life Forum

supported by roads, water networks and drains. Occupation of areas originally devoted to parks, gardens and other social uses weakened initial plans and the city grew in a disorderly way, creating problems that affect the quality of life of current inhabitants. It is estimated that today nearly 70 per cent of the city population live in areas characterized by deficient water services, pollution and disease.

The recent implementation of Local Agenda 21 in Nuevo Chimbote has meant the beginning of highly participatory processes striving to generate sustainable human development and the reinforcement of democratic transition at a local level. In these processes, a key role has been played by the creation of alliances and support brought by a private–public, inter-institutional network called the Cities for Life Forum. The Forum has ushered in the development of a self-diagnosis that has resulted in a shared socio-economic and environmental vision. A series of activities with children, young people, women and public and private institutions were developed in order to validate this shared vision of the future, which was subsequently approved and signed by local actors.

The Cities for Life Forum is an unprecedented initiative in Peru. It works for the promotion of democratic civic practices and unites efforts and local resources in order to design a new logic of sustainable development that:

☐ incorporates top-down and bottom-up actions;
☐ integrates social development, economic development and environmental management;
☐ promotes a planning culture with long-term perspective and practical short-term actions;
☐ channels state and private sector funds on the basis of participatory budgeting and applies the principle of shared responsibility among public and private actors.

In order to achieve all this, the Cities for Life Forum promotes and strengthens:

☐ coordination among public actors and civil society;
☐ consensus-building among municipalities;
☐ the value of local spaces as the stage for development planning and management;
☐ connectivity between areas within the region;
☐ an inter-institutional forum;
☐ a cross-disciplinary and cross-sector approach.

Despite successes in changing attitudes and perceptions in the region, struggles continue to institutionalize policy mechanisms ensuring the long-term successes of the Cities for Life Forum. For example, because there is not a formal process of monitoring at governmental level, many member NGOs are making efforts to disseminate all of their lessons learned so that processes, results and outcomes can be evaluated and refined. Liliana Miranda, Executive Director of the Cities for Life Forum and founder of the NGO Ecociudad, explains that a number of generic skills are facilitating a shared monitoring and evaluation process and its mainstreaming into more widespread use. In addition to the necessary skills of patience, perseverance, joy, tolerance, temper, honesty and ethics Ms Miranda cites for engaging others, she sees collaboration, listening, pragmatism and the ability to accept and learn from mistakes as key elements to success and a type of monitoring and evaluation that will lead to more productive ends.

Source:
Liliana Miranda

Contact:
Liliana Miranda
Vargas Machuca 408 San
Antonio Miraflores Lima
Tel/fax: +51-1-2411488,
2425140
e-mail:
lmiranda@ciudad.org.pe
Website: www.ciudad.org.pe

This case study makes two important points. First, it is not uncommon for exciting, highly participatory projects to grow without much thought being given to formal evaluation and systems to deliver structured learning. The energy that drives activism may come from different genes than the rational calculating mind that asks for facts and figures and performance measurement. Good monitoring needs both sets of qualities. Second, it is important to attempt to make monitoring and evaluation a shared and open process. As Ms.Miranda implies, this demands some rather different skills than designing a questionnaire and then ticking boxes. Debate and confrontation with different views and interpretations is likely to create a deeper form of learning than more superficial means of measuring outputs.

7.2 Learning from and with others

The value of learning through 'horizontal' peer-group exchanges is becoming widely understood. Not only is it generally extremely effective in terms of its capacity to introduce new ideas in a credible and acceptable way, but it is also efficient in terms of cost and direct impact. Being able to discuss different experiences in comparable situations with peers, despite differences in cultural backgrounds, is infinitely more convincing and therefore acceptable than is possible with many more traditional approaches to training. Seeing and being able to discuss at first-hand the problems and successes of development programmes and projects gives them a credibility that is hard to convey through courses and textbooks. (This is why this guide provides contacts for each of the case studies.)

The following two case studies describe peer-group exchanges in different circumstances, the first at the level of regional policy and planning authorities in Northern Europe, the second between slum NGOs and federations of slum dwellers in Asia and Africa.

The European Union has actively promoted schemes whereby regional and municipal authorities (and other partners) cooperate through working together on projects that encompass common concerns. Case Study 23 gives an examples of how new skills can be learned through such collaborations.

Case Study 23: EUROPE

The Innovation Circle

The Baltic Sea region includes some of the most remote rural areas in Europe, in Sweden, Finland and Norway. The region also includes Poland, and Estonia, Latvia and Lithuania, countries which were part of the USSR from the 1940s to the early 1990s. Rural regions and small towns outside the capital cities in all these countries are losing young people who go to large cities for higher education then do not return home after graduating. There are few facilities for higher education in many of these regions.

Ageing and dwindling populations are less innovative than young populations with many new-comers and outsiders. A cycle of decline is a real risk, with loss of jobs and services accelerating out-migration. Officials working in small towns in sparsely populated areas can easily feel isolated. Similarly, officials who spent the formative years of their working life in public service in the USSR, where local government had little autonomy, are less likely to have the skills needed to deliver today's public services.

Under the leadership of Alytus municipality (Lithuania) 12 other councils and civil society bodies including some from Russia have got together to develop a programme of collaborative learning on the theme of innovation. The learning takes place through reading distance learning materials specially commissioned by the project, covering themes that include competitiveness, governance and participation, sustainable design, business development and project management. There are face-to-face workshops that support the development of skills linked to the reading. Ideas are then put into practice through projects delivered locally but in partnership with other members of the Innovation Circle. Last but not least there are summer camps for young people, where they also learn about innovation and become more aware of the positive features of their home towns and regions and the scope for getting involved in their future. Outreach to involve youths is a key theme in the project.

The backgrounds of those taking part are varied. As well as a minority who are professional planners or architects, there are teachers, cultural workers, youth workers, administrators, politicians and some people from the business sector. There is a strong emphasis on skills of creativity, team working, planning and good governance. Partners are able to benchmark themselves against others and pick up new ideas. A project website also keeps people in touch though they live far apart and provides a resource for all partners.

Source:
Inese Suija

Contact:
The Baltic Innovation Group
Website: www.big@baltic-innovation.lt

© Baltic Innovation Group

This project shows how skills can be developed through inter-organizational and inter-professional learning and applied in partnership. The networks draw on the experiences of member organizations to develop knowledge about how best to act in places with similar conditions and problems.

Case Study 24 describes an exchange methodology to strengthen the capacity of local grassroots organizations to devise new development alternatives, be recognized by municipalities for their work, and scale-up community innovations from project to city and from practice to policy.

Case Study 24: SHACK DWELLERS INTERNATIONAL

Learning through community exchange

This case study considers the experience of national urban poor federations and their support NGOs that make up the international network of Shack or Slum Dwellers International (SDI) for learning and knowledge sharing between communities.

Each member federation is made up of local community organizations carrying out savings schemes in which women play a key role. The primary goal of the federations is to develop the capacities of urban poor communities so that they build strong organizations that can articulate needs and aspirations, have the capacity and confidence to design and manage solutions that can be scaledup and seek to participate in development activities as partners rather than as beneficiaries. To this end, they have developed a set of tools exchanged between communities for 'peer learning'. This consists of members from different communities within a city, a country or internationally visiting each other to meet and exchange ideas, experiences and the methods they have developed over time.

Community exchanges serve many purposes. They spread 'knowledge capital' built on the urban poor communities' own experiences – for instance, how to set up saving schemes, how to give and manage loans, how to collect and manage household and housing data, and how to manage land, building and relations with local authorities. Community exchanges are also a means of drawing large numbers of people into a process of change, supporting local reflection and analysis, enabling the urban poor to own the process of knowledge creation and providing a catalyst for taking their actions and learning process a step forward. Exchanges enable the poor to reach out and federate, thereby developing a collective vision and collective strength. They help create strong personal bonds between communities that share common problems, both presenting them with a range of options to choose from and negotiate for and assuring them that they are not alone in their struggle. Through interaction with their peers and a better understanding of the process of change that has taken place in other settlements, community leaders learn to position themselves as drivers within larger scale development processes. Finally, they are a way to influence the professionals and members of governments who get invited to join in these community exchanges. This opens space for negotiation and encourages other actors involved in urban development to adjust their perspectives of the poor and consider the innovations and experimentation that they have undertaken. By expanding exchanges between urban poor organizations to the international level, the SDI network also seeks to demonstrate to international agencies the learning that these community exchanges produce.

A community exchange in Namibia, with participants from the South African and

© Homeless International

Photo:
Slum dwellers from India and Uganda preparing a joint 'model house' ehhibition (in Uganda).

Contact:
Shack Dwellers International
Website:
http://www.sdinet.org

Zimbabwean federations, illustrates the learning produced by the experience for each party. For the South Africans, it was a chance to explore in more detail the policy of incremental infrastructure development in Windhoek that had developed from a partnership between the Namibian federation and the city authorities. For the Zimbabweans, it was a way of spreading a better understanding of the policy of incremental development within their federation and with their support NGO (Dialogue on Shelters). It also proved an opportunity to explore appropriate professional support strategies within the group. For the Namibians, it offered an opportunity to assess the technical strengths and weaknesses of their work in installing infrastructure. The federations also gained more information on how their work was perceived and what might usefully be addressed.

Central to the concept of learning through community exchange is the recognition that most community members who have not gone through a formal education system have very different ways of collecting and synthesizing knowledge. They learn through real life experiences what works and what does not and have collective wisdom, rather than written documents, seminars and educational meetings organized by professionals. The knowledge that people, especially the very poor, have created forms the basis of their survival strategies. By enabling communities to share and explore such knowledge, the poor get to realize that they can help play a definitive role in development processes. As the links between communities become stronger and as more people experiment with this new learning, ideas are refined and put into practice, use is scaled-up and replication and adaptation take place.

A condition for community exchanges to be successful is that communities undertaking exchanges are linked together in a network or federation. This ensures that the solutions that are explored and elaborated are those that emerge from the communities' own experience in addressing poverty and that make sense to a large number of urban poor communities with the potential to be embedded in community practice and scaled-up. Leadership is another important factor, as it is the regional and national leaders that keep in touch with the many communities that participate in the process and ensures that communities are organized and mobilized so as to be able to exert political influence. Finally, it is important that there remains very little or no professional intervention in the community learning process. The poor are much more committed to the solutions – even if they take a very long time – if they see that change is possible using their own strategies and processes and is aimed at priorities they have set themselves.

7.3 Learning in practice

Even when exchanges and international projects are not possible, skills can be learned from local practice. The skill of learning occurs and affects action in a variety of ways and from a variety of sources. Learning from mistakes is a form of good practice! The case of Kumasi, Ghana illustrates the potential gains of recognizing and addressing faults in plans for intervention at an early stage. In this case, reflection steered planners away from a path with less potential and opened up a new one with many more opportunities. By broadening the scope of input contributing to its work, the International Water Management Institute (IWMI), added different experience and

Further information:
D'Cruz, C. and Mitlin, D. (n.d.) Shack/Slum Dwellers International: One Experience of the Contribution of Membership Organizations to Pro-poor Urban Development, International Institute for Environment and Development (IIED), Institute for Development Policy and Management (IDPM) University of Manchester, downloadable from the IIED website: http://www.iied.org/HS/documents/SDI_membership_orgs05.pdf
Patel, S., Bolnick, J. and Mitlin, D. (n.d.) Sharing Experiences and Changing Lives, document downloadable from: http://www.theinclusivecity.org/resources/research_papers/SharingPaper_main.htm
Shack Dwellers International website: http://www.sdinet.org ; in particular, see the Report 4 'Face to face: A comprehensive detailed discussion of the ideas, practices, and results of horizontal or community-to–community exchanges within the SDI network'.

knowledge to its team and augmented the capacity of this project to make a positive long-term impact. Furthermore, in partnering with local universities, IWMI increased its potential for analysis and influence from the more academic side of planning.

Case Study 25: GHANA

Learning from rapid urban growth and reflection in Kumasi

There is great potential for recycling nutrients from organic city waste for use in agriculture. In researching the potential for the utilization of techniques to this end, early estimates for the city of Kumasi, Ghana, by the Urban Agriculture Group of the International Water Management Institute indicated that only 10 per cent of the major plant nutrients entering the city were being reclaimed and attempts to apply food waste recycling were problematic due to numerous technical, marketing and institutional problems in composting stations.

To help address this problem, IWMI undertook to analyse nutrient flows across the rural–urban interface and to develop recycling strategies to close the nutrient cycle and preserve the quality of the urban environment. Initial phases of IWMI's work revealed that:

☐ there was sufficient organic waste of good quality for composting as well as options for successful community involvement in the operation of compost stations;

☐ the willingness to pay of the majority of interested farmers was too low to cover the running costs of the compost stations. Because only those farmers with higher than average means and willingness to pay could afford compost, it was estimated that the production limit (and nutrient recycling) would be reduced to about 10 per cent of the total annual compost demand unless subsidies were provided;

☐ those who could afford the compost were mostly located in the peri-urban area. Thus, subsidies could best be justified if compost production took place in peri-urban towns not yet connected to urban waste collection. Here, composting would be closer to the farmers and local waste dumps would be given significant relief, so funds otherwise spent on the transport of waste would be saved.

Before trying to develop decision support on composting and exploring institutional components to recycling strategies in subsequent stages of its work, IWMI chose to study existing compost stations in the West African subregion to learn from the experiences of other projects. Very few compost stations were found to be even close to levels that could be considered sustainable. What was more, IWMI discovered that institutionally and financially, the compost stations were not viable. At this point, project leaders realized that their technical approach had inaccurately addressed challenges of urbanization and that the mainly agricultural scope of research being done was too narrow.

Source:
Pay Drechsel

Contact:
Pay Drechsel
International Water
Management Institute
(IWMI)
P.M.B. CT 112
Accra, GhanaTel: +233-21-
784753/4
Fax: +233-21-784752
e-mail: p.drechsel@cgiar.org
Website:
www.iwmi.org/africa/west_
africa

To improve its capacity to tackle a wider approach, IWMI strengthened its team, forming alliances with 15 different university departments of three national universities. Over 100 students were incorporated into the research and joined IWMI seminars and field interviews. The result was a significant rise in the levels of monitoring and feedback coming back to the project coordinating unit and an increase in the project's ability to react quickly to new information.

© IWMI

In addition, by adding a vast field of input to their work, IWMI augmented both the technical and non-technical skills available to it. Now part of the team were researchers qualified in planning, institutional analysis, economics, engineering, participatory research and environmental science. Through its partnerships, IWMI became increasingly adaptable and open to learn in its approach.

Continuing today, IWMI's work in Ghana maintains flexibility and is strengthened by curiosity and an organizational framework that incorporates new ideas easily. While its focus remains on technical innovations in recycling solid and liquid urban waste, IWMI's incorporation of contextually based and institutionally aware research into its work has resulted in the greater relevance and perspective of its findings. Despite having faced numerous barriers in its work, IWMI attributes its continued progress to its ability to think creatively and respond to change.

7.4 Being a 'reflective' practitioner

At a more personal level, monitoring must relate to planning as a profession, planners and the organizations for which they work. As a skill, this means looking at what can be learned from one's individual perceptions and actions and how they relate to a particular context or intervention.

Planners have got to re-evaluate the notion of 'expertise' as it relates to their work by seeing and acknowledging greater, personal limitations and assumptions. They must make these limits known to their clients and colleagues so that grey areas can be explored, collaboration can occur and unanswered questions can begin to be more directly addressed. Donald Schön suggests this idea in his concept of 'the reflective practitioner'. Schön observes that the benefit of having this 'reflective' attitude, wherein one looks not only outward but inward as well, is that 'when a practitioner becomes a researcher into his own practice, he engages in a continuing process of self-education'.

In practice, being reflective carries with it strong connections to context. Time and flexibility to think, learn or collaborate can be restricted, particularly because in a vast majority of cases, planning professionals have duties that demand tangible results rather than evidence of reflection. Roles for individuals must be managed with reference to contracts, professional codes of conduct or other working guidelines. While bearing their other obligations in mind, planners must not lose sight of the fact that they have a responsibility to manage themselves and their relations with others. In this respect, self-monitoring skills for planners can include questioning of their own work, guidelines applied to their practices or goals, and actions of their organizations with respect to their personal ethics.

Organizations can support a reflective, ethical way of working with a transparent, flexible and flat management structure. Planning bodies, like individual planners, need to listen, promote leadership, celebrate success, work as a team and value each of their members in order to provide improved results. Furthermore, they must look beyond the confines of their everyday operations to find new approaches, theoretical, methodological and practical, that relate to their work. To be part of lasting change, organizations need to demonstrate a willingness to maintain involvement and, even in technical interventions, the awareness that changing structures but not institutions will likely result in the achievement of very little.

The way knowledge, experience, assumptions and limitations are incorporated will ultimately affect the potential of intervention to achieve change. Being reflective at an individual and organizational level provides planning with a way to develop more positive practices and more viable solutions. In support of this notion, the following case studies are brief reflections by three planners engaged in planning education and research, in consultancy and an NGO.

Case Study 26: BEING REFLECTIVE IN PRACTICE

Education and research

The director of a UK university planning centre considers that strategic reflection is a key aspect of what planners and related institutions need to do to legitimize professional activities and maintain these as close as possible to strategic objectives. In his role as an educator, this means drawing on what he has gained as an individual through life and work experiences as well as secondary sources, for example, through reading and discussion, and then incorporating this into his students' education so it can be passed on, challenged or developed further. As a researcher, he sees great significance in how acting as a reflective practitioner assists in essential understanding of the context for development research and the learning that occurs between NGOs, research centres and other actors. He cites as an example of this approach to knowledge development and dissemination the dialogue and collaborative learning developed by his centre and partner organizations in the United Kingdom, Angola and Mozambique. He considers that contextual analysis and collaborative research development are skills that are crucial aspects of a proactive professional approach.

Case Study 27: BEING REFLECTIVE IN PRACTICE

Consultant

As a British consultant who has spent much of his career in the field overseas, he sees great importance in emphasizing what reflection means in a practical sense. In his experience, reflection involves sharing and using personal experiences to recognize the specific characteristics of contexts and derive tangible solutions. This collaboratively based reflection is crucial to planners in their efforts to diagnose situations and recognize what potential solutions planning might offer. Although he sees value in innovation and imagination, he sees these ideas as lacking significant connections with what really happens on the ground in many interventions. He emphasizes that under pressures from time and/or clients, planners in the field have few luxuries, therefore limiting the option to explore every avenue through research and analysis. In working efficiently and realistically towards the satisfaction of obligations, being imaginative means concentrating on doing and combining more of the things that planners know will work. In this respect and because local conditions are unique, reflection that draws on experience to find workable solutions is most effective when it incorporates the combined knowledge of all stakeholders involved.

Case Study 28: BEING REFLECTIVE IN PRACTICE

NGO

Working in the tsunami-stricken district of Kanyakumari in southern India, he is exploring the meaning and limits of reflection in everyday work. As a project manager for a Paris-based NGO, he believes that being reflective means being professionally humble, maintaining a close check on the limits of expertise and exploring insights from different knowledge in a process of adapting actions to specific contexts. In India, however, faced with the pressures of time and aid recipients eager to have new homes, reflection must entail collaboration with colleagues and communities so

© Emilie malbec/Architecture et development

that underlying interests are exposed, relevant experiences are brought into planning actions and workable, forward-looking solutions are developed. In his experience dealing with disaster recovery, he finds that the benefits of being reflective are immense. Actors involved in reconstruction efforts have valued results more and adapted quicker to the local context. Furthermore, he asserts that through reflection, the solutions being implemented in Kanyakumari are the most appropriate for this recovering community to gain greater capacity in future development efforts.

7.5 Summary

This chapter has argued that learning is vital but can take many different forms. Learning skills are also varied but include:

- ☐ the ability to identify needs in relation to information, knowledge and skills;
- ☐ the ability to devise and manage formal systems for monitoring outputs and performance;
- ☐ the ability to learn collaboratively with and from others;
- ☐ the ability to use distance learning materials to steer learning, especially for those in locations that are remote from centres offering face-to-face tuition;
- ☐ the ability to be a reflective practitioner.

Key lessons

- ☐ **Innovation is essential if planning practices are to make an impact for more sustainable forms of urban development.**

- ☐ **Learning is essential for innovation.**

- ☐ **Planning and innovation are not linear processes; they depend on contact with multiple sources of information and ideas, both inside and outside the organizations. Critical reflection on practice is fundamental to achieving improvements and developing new skills.**

Section 3

THE WAY AHEAD

Section 3
THE WAY AHEAD

This short section reflects on some of the ideas in the preceding chapters. It raises several questions. What are the implications of getting to grips with the sorts of skill sets outlined in Section 2? Can they and should they be institutionalized by urban planners and managers? What does it mean for the planning profession and planning education systems?

8 New places, new planning, new skills?

The problems of urban growth and the urbanization of poverty that are outlined in Section 1 are are becoming familiar internationally. The response, however, is often one of resignation and inertia in the face of their seemingly insurmountable scale. The benefits and opportunities of urbanization, also described in Section 1, receive less attention and can easily be overlooked, even by people who themselves benefit from urban lifestyles and livelihoods.

Many examples given in Section 2 show how problems of urban development can be turned into opportunities. They provide an insight into approaches and practices for the planning and management of towns and cities that build upon the potentials and resources (most of them human) that are provided by the process of urbanization itself. They also describe the sorts of skills that can make a difference when combined with the efforts and energies of people and institutions. Many of the skills have been learnt through practice and were not part of traditional professional training.

There was never an intention to present the case studies in Section 2 as 'best practices', and many of them show what can go wrong as well as what works. Nevertheless, taken together they make an optimistic narrative. They also show that, while conditions vary widely between the rich countries of the global North and the poorer countries of the South, many of the generic skills required for more sustainable settlements are very similar.

This is not a prescription for their direct and uncritical adoption in other situations. Local conditions, resources and cultures must be filters on transfers – adaptations will always be necessary and are entirely legitimate. However, it is suggested that globalization in its many guises is posing some very similar challenges in different places. Cities are spreading and putting pressure on the environment, the gap between rich and poor is widening, governments are weaker and need to work with other partners, international networking opens new possibilities, and above all, the barriers of social exclusion need to be broken down. The experiences outlined in the preceding chapters show that urban planning and management need to change, have changed and are changing.

8.1 Changing places, changing skills, changing planning

Despite these general observations, the quantitative and qualitative changes that are happening in settlements and regions have not yet been fully comprehended, even by many planners who, perhaps more than any other single profession, should be engrossed in urban analysis. It is these changes that are driving the people who contributed to our case studies, and many more like them, to try to find new ways of working, new relationships between governments and civil society, and new skills.

Many of the skills now needed are fundamental to a planning process: collecting and analyzing information, managing competing demands, creating visions for the future, monitoring and evaluation are all examples. Indeed there will be some who argue that Section 2 is not about new skills at all, but a reassertion of traditional planning skills, albeit sometimes in new settings and with new emphases. However, the novelty really lies in the extent to which active engagement and networking with very diverse groups and individuals, and proactive consensus building amid conditions where conflict is often deep rooted, are seen as fundamental to achieving more equitable and sustainable development and to everything planners do.

Thus urban planning cannot be separated from the management of urban development or the administration of urban services. It is ironic, however, that urban planning as a profession is still often demarcated by a concern only with the location and distribution of land uses and the control of its development, and is seen as almost exclusively based in the public sector. The double irony is that this marginalization of planning means that an integrated and practical approach to human settlements has also been marginalized. There are signs that this is beginning to change. The planning and management of urban development embraces a great deal more than land use. Those engaged in urban development have roles to play in the political process of decision making, the managerial functions of implementing development policies, programmes and projects, and intervening in the day-to-day administration of infrastructure and service delivery.

The extent to which different actors have separate roles principally depends on the human resources that are available. In a wealthy Northern city a relatively high degree of professional and technical specialization may be expected, but in many towns and cities of the South one or two public sector professionals, who may or may not be planners, often have to take responsibility for a wide range of issues. These not only span the processes of planning, management and administration, but also entail operating at a variety of different levels: for instance with policy makers and politicians; donors and aid agents; technical and professional consultants; civil society and faith-based organizations; community leaders and local political groups; private enterprises and associations; and their peers in other departments of the administration – health, education, works and so on.

Thus, in addition to developing the sorts of skills outlined in the chapters in Section 2, urban planners and managers, particularly those in countries with a scarcity of professionals and technicians, have to have at least a basic understanding of many different disciplines: civil engineering and the extension and maintenance of infrastructure; urban design and the use of public land; environmental health and conservation; land management and property markets; urban sociology and community development; urban economics and public revenue management; municipal law and development control standards and legislation.

This is not to say that urban planners and managers replace the need for all other professionals. Rather it shows that, especially in situations of rapid urbanization and few skilled staff, professionalism has to become more generic. The old professionalism was about excluding outsiders and erecting boundary fences around knowledge and skills. This is the very antithesis to conditions now known to foster creative thought and innovation. Professionals need to share their knowledge and skills with each other and with non-professionals with whom and for whom they work. The more barriers they cross the more likely it is that the outcomes will contribute towards sustainable settlements.

8.2 Where next?

Most planners and planning researchers and academics are in rich countries that are far removed in almost every way from the less developed countries where 93 per cent of the increase in the world's urban population is expected to take place over the next 15 years. There is not only a gross spatial maldistribution of professional planners, there is an urgent need for a transformation in capacity for the governance, planning and management of settlements globally.

This implies quantitative change – many more people with the right knowledge and skills – and qualitative change, which means identifying and developing key skills. Local knowledge and understanding will always be vital to the good governance of human settlements, and the nature of governance will be shaped by different traditions and cultures. However, it should be possible to modernize planning through globalizing the knowledge and skills networks and in particular through finding ways to develop capacity quickly in those places where the pool of skills in urban planning has not kept pace with the rate of urbanization.

Capacity building, however, is not only a question of developing skills, important though they are. If the development of appropriately equipped professionals is to be made more effective by training and encouraging them to operate in different ways and in conjunction with different partners, they need responsive and supportive organizational environments in which to exercise their new understanding and skills. However, many local government departments, in which many planners work, are structured in ways and with traditions that do to not allow new initiatives or encourage inter-agency collaboration or cooperation with civil society and community groups. Thus, simultaneous changes in the organizational structures, particularly of local government, are needed in order to allow new approaches to planning and management to flourish. But the ability of government departments and agencies to change is often constrained by higher level national institutions, legislation and regulations. Thus, institutional change, that entails national-level political and legislative intervention, is also simultaneously required.

In addition to the three components of capacity building – institutional development, organizational development and human resource development – the ability to increase the relevance and effectiveness of urban planning and management is constrained where professional education has not been modernized, opportunities for continuing professional development are limited or non-existent, and traditions of professionalism are defensive and exclusionary. Formal education and professionalism have a vital role to play in delivering the kind of approaches and skills that this guide has identified but they are only part of the picture. Sub-professional training, training the trainers, accreditation of experiential learning (the know-how picked up in civil society organizations, for example) and continuing professional development are of paramount importance.

Much could be achieved if the international community, governments, professional associations and higher education institutions worked together to actively promote more inclusive and participatory approaches, such as those outlined in Section 2, and to ensure that access to appropriate skills was easily available in places where they are urgently needed. The mandate for this was given by the Istanbul Declaration and Habitat Agenda, endorsed by 171 member states at the United Nations City Summit a decade ago.

At the same time, there is a range of more immediate and pragmatic actions that need to be taken at different levels. Important among these are:

☐ Making better and more effective use of the internet to spread and build knowledge and to forge new networks and exchanges of experience between professionals and all others engaged in integrated and participatory approaches to sustainable urban planning and management and poverty reduction. It is often pointed out that in many situations not even professionals, or the institutions and agencies in which they work, have access to the internet or the technical and language skills to benefit from it. However, this situation is changing extremely rapidly and it should certainly not be used as an excuse for inertia. Nevertheless, imagination is still needed to develop ways to publicize appropriate websites and to make them easier to understand, use and interact with.

☐ Greater investment in the development and delivery of affordable and accessible distance learning opportunities for appropriate planning-related education and skill training. Where possible, such programmes should also carry credits towards the award of recognized qualifications, not only to provide incentives, but also to legitimize their beneficiaries professionally in order to help advance them on their local career ladder and to add weight to the content of the alternative education and training that they provide.

☐ More coherent approaches and proliferation of training on-the-job, for-the-job and by-the-job that help build structures that encourage and support the 'reflective practitioner', and create ladders of opportunity for those outside professions, but who are actively engaged in trying to manage urban change in sustainable ways. Such training support is increasingly becoming part of international planning consultancy contracts and NGO activities in countries of the South, but it needs reinforcing and extending to a wider range of support agencies. As with distance learning, it needs to receive greater formal recognition and legitimization.

☐ Increased networking and combined pressure and support by the international profes sional bodies and associations to raise the political profile of urban issues and the urgent need for a significant change in the level of political commitment and investment in all three components of capacity building. Many international profes sional associations, partners in the Governing Council of the United Nations Human Settlements Programme, are already committed to this end, but their ranks can grow and their efforts can be redoubled.

☐ Encouraging greater media awareness and popular publicity to the success stories and related messages concerning the impact of more participatory approaches to the development of settlements, such as those in Section 2 of this guide. The power of public pressure on policy and procedural reform, in whatever political system, cannot be underestimated. However, people need positive and progressive examples in order to develop visions and make demands of their leaders, but virtually all of the current press coverage and commentary on urban growth and change is negative, alarmist and doom-laden. Good news needs to be made newsworthy.

As with all the messages in this guide, these exhortations are not new. The have been made before and they are all already being implemented in many places by many people. However, if the Millennium Development Goals are to be met, in urban and rural areas alike there will have to be a quantum shift to more sustainable approaches to the planning and management of settlements in the coming half-decade. This will not be easy but it can be done.

GLOSSARY

GLOSSARY

CAPACITY BUILDING

To many people capacity building means training or human resource development. Certainly this is a very major component of it. However, if decision makers, managers, professionals and technicians are to operate at full capacity, they need more than just their own abilities. They need a conducive and supportive institutional and organizational environment. Therefore to be effective capacity building must embrace all three aspects:

Human resource development (HRD) is the process of equipping people with the understanding and skills, and the access to information and knowledge to perform effectively. It includes motivating people to operate constructively and efficiently through the development of positive attitudes and progressive approaches to responsibility and productivity. Good human resource management provides incentives and rewards; opportunities for continuous training and retraining; clearly recognizable career opportunities; and competitive pay scales. To achieve these aspects of HRD, the organizational environment must be dynamic and responsive.

Organizational development is the process that promotes and sustains collective activity within an organization. It is to do with management practices and procedures; rules and regulations; hierarchies and job descriptions – the structures and practices that shape how things get done. It is also to do with working relationships; shared goals and values; teamwork, dependencies and supports – why things get done. The increasing demand for more flexible and responsive management styles calls for organizational structures and relationships that will ingrain such practices; particularly within local government such structures and relationships might require significant changes. Organizational development also calls for new relationships between different organizations that have a role in urban planning and management. However, bringing about such organizational changes often depends upon institutional changes that are beyond the capacity of any single organization or network of organizations.

Institutional development encompasses the legal and regulatory changes that have to be made in order to enable organizations, institutions and agencies at all levels and in all sectors to enhance their capacities. It embraces such issues as regulations controlling the financial management, the borrowing and trading capacity of municipal authorities; the ability of local government to negotiate contracts and form partnerships with private enterprises and community organizations; centrally regulated conditions of employment, salaries and career structures; land use and building bylaws, and other development controls; and democratic legislation that allows, enables and encourages communities to take responsibility for the management of their own neighbourhoods and services. Such institutional issues generally need the political and legislative authority of national government to bring about effective change.

COMMUNICATION SKILLS

Communication is a process of giving and receiving information. Because everyone communicates it is easy to assume that communication skills can be taken for granted. However, the difference between good and bad communication can hugely affect the success of plans and projects. **Listening skills** in particular are often undervalued. It is important to listen to what community spokespersons or other stakeholders are actually saying – not what you presume they will say. Understanding body language may also be part of 'listening'. **Presentation skills** also take different forms. These include writing in a way that makes it easy for others, especially non-professionals, to understand. Public speaking skills are important also. Interaction is important in communication and an interactive style of delivery is likely to hold attention better than a long monologue. These are just a few examples of skills that can be quickly learned. Visual images can be powerful means of communication and may be valuable in situations where language is a barrier. Role play is an extremely valuable way to help people understand different experiences and points of view. Sometimes **marketing skills** are needed to mobilize support for projects or ideas, to open minds to new possibilities or to sustain support through difficult times.

COMMUNITY

Community has many meanings and connotations, but for the purposes of this guide it is a local group of (low-income) households that identify themselves in some way or other as having a common interest or bond – values, resources and needs as well as physical space. It is common for planners to refer to all the people living in a particular neighbourhood as a 'community'. However, most urban communities are also socially diverse and embrace subgroups with values and aspirations, different access to resources and power. So, in dealing with community leaders care must always be taken to ensure that they represent the whole community and that there are not marginalized groups who are being left out or exploited.

CSO, NGO and CBO

Civil society organizations (CSOs) are all organized and constituted groups that are not agencies or departments of government or the profit-making private commercial and industrial sector. CSOs embrace registered charities, trade unions, faith-based organizations, foundations, community groups, women's organizations, professional associations, self-help groups, social movements, business associations, coalitions and advocacy groups. It is a loose term that includes NGOs and CBOs.

Non-governmental organizations (NGOs) is also a somewhat general catch-all term. However, in recent years it has become identified with non-profit organizations that champion and support particular social causes such as human rights, the environment, gender equity, heritage conservation, combating HIV/AIDS. NGOs may broadly be categorized as non-governmental development organizations (NGDOs) that typically raise funds in the richer countries of the North to support development work related to their cause in the

South, and local NGOs that tend to work closely with community groups. Many local NGOs in the South have links to international NGOs that provide much of their funding, while many of those in the North are linked particular to government welfare programmes as well as raising their own charitable funds.

Community-based organizations (CBOs) differ from NGOs in that their principal concerns are with all aspects of the welfare and development of a particular community. They are not cause-specific and their area of operation is geographically defined. Few urban communities are entirely homogeneous and frequently CBOs do not represent all of the households in a particular area, which can lead to conflict or to the marginalization of sub-groups.

DEVOLUTION and DECENTRALIZATION

Devolution is the handing down of policy and major decision-making powers and authority to a lower level of governance – from central to local government; from a municipal council to ward level or neighbourhood committees. It entails a transfer of power, which many people in authority are reluctant to do, but also means transferring responsibility for failures as well as successes – a more attractive proposition.

Decentralization is the process of transferring responsibility from central agencies and institutions to lower levels of management and administration. It does not necessarily entail the devolution of policy decisions; responsibility for the implementation of policy can be decentralized without transferring authority. Other terms such as **delegation**, deconcentration, decongestion are alternative terms that are frequently used to describe forms of decentralization and devolution by governments in order to share responsibilities with other levels of *governance* under the principle of *subsidiarity*.

DIVERSITY and INCLUSION

Social diversity is the recognition of the social relations that underpin the many different groups and communities that make up society in urban areas. In particular it draws attention to social exclusion, or those who in one way or another are marginalized from the benefits of development either because they are actively discriminated against or because they are 'invisible' or have no 'voice'. Policies directed at *poverty alleviation* often fall short by assuming that 'the urban poor' is a homogenous group and all will benefit from a single strategy, which is very rarely the case. Different groups, on the basis of their class, gender, age, ethnicity, religion and physical/mental ability, have different demands and perceptions and offer different attributes to urban society, all of which need to be heard and responded to. The most widespread challenge to diversity is that of the different *gender needs and roles* of women and men, discussed below.

Social inclusion is not only about people having a say in the planning, maintenance and management of the environments in which they live and the institutions that deal with them directly. Real inclusion is reached when people can access all the institutions and assets of the city – access local political decision making, the banking system, understand the jobs market, negotiate their children's education and so on. See also 'Equality'.

EMPOWERING and ENABLING

Empowering and enabling are central to processes of *devolution* and *decentralization*. **Empowering** means giving authority to an institution or organization (or individual) to determine policy and make decisions. It is about *inclusion* and bringing people who are outside the decision-making process into it.

Enabling means providing the resources (professional, technical, financial and so on) and access to knowledge that ensure that an institution or organization (or individual) has the capacity and skills to exercise its responsibility effectively and efficiently. Government sponsored enabling strategies for the production low-income housing, such as *sites and service* schemes for instance, entail the identification of what supports are needed by a particular group of beneficiaries that will enable them to exercise their responsibilities (constructing their dwellings themselves or supervising their contractors or artisans) effectively and efficiently.

ENGAGEMENT

Engagement means entering into a deliberative process of dialogue with others, actively seeking and listening to their views and exchanging ideas, information and opinions. Such dialogue is likely to be necessary to build a platform of mutual confidence and understanding so that *empowering and enabling* become possible. Engagement should be inclusive and recognize that past practices and exclusion may have left barriers that have to be overcome to achieve mutual understanding. Engagement can be a way to identify stakeholders and clarify interests, conflicts and the scope for building consensus. Formal public participation programmes can easily be dominated by 'the usual suspects' – that is the same articulate and well organized bodies that have developed skills in working with public bodies to ensure their views are heard. Unless there is *outreach*, to engage other groups, such participation processes can reproduce social exclusion and inequality of opportunity.

EQUITY and EQUALITY

Equity is the quality of being impartial and 'fair' in the distribution of the benefits and costs of development and the provision of access to opportunities for all. It is not the same as **equality**. Treating everybody the same is unlikely to be equitable if people have different needs and opportunities to begin with. An understanding of *diversity* is likely to promote equity, as it recognizes how poverty, disability, age, gender and such like, influence access to needs and opportunities within settlements. Equality and equality require such understanding, but also skills such as the ability to undertake equality impact assessments to analyze the effect that a policy or procedure will have on a particular group of people, and to explore whether their needs are being met, or whether there are unintended discriminatory effects and outcomes. Where inequalities are deep-rooted and/or past discrimination needs to be overcome, positive action may be necessary, involving, for example, the setting of targets and the mobilization of resources to narrow the gaps.

GENDER NEEDS and ROLES

Gender, in the context of settlement planning and management, is understanding and responding to the different needs, and social roles and relations of women and men. Both play multiple roles in society. Broadly in most societies women tend to have primary respon-sibility for reproductive roles, be involved in productive and community management roles, and they may also be involved in political roles, though often only as rank and file members. In most societies, men tend to be involved in particular in productive or political roles, more often than women in senior management or leadership roles respectively, and they generally play them sequentially. In contrast, women generally have to play their roles simultaneously, balancing the competing claims on time for each. In general, women and men have different levels of both access to the resources needed for their work, and control over those resources.

Gender mainstreaming is the process of ensuring that women and men have equal access and control over resources, development benefits and decision making, at all stages of the development process.

Gender planning refers to the processes of planning that are gender sensitive and take into account the impact of differing gender roles, gender relations and the gender needs of women and men in a development programme or project in ways that are continuous and sustainable in order to achieve gender mainstreaming. It involves the selection of appropriate approaches to address women and men's practical gender needs and to identify and challenge inequitable relations and allocations of resources or benefits.

GENERIC SKILLS

These are skills that are not unique to any single profession or discipline. Rather they are skills that many different professions and also non-professionals need. They include skills such as communication, management, negotiation and so on.

GOVERNANCE

Governance is the process of making decisions and monitoring their implementation. Good governance is the process of decision making that recognizes, respects and engages all the potential actors and *stakeholders* who will be affected by the decisions that are made. Therefore it is inclusive and participatory, involving and bringing together actors from central government (notably service delivery agencies – health, education and so on), local government (both political decision makers and technical and administrative officers), civil society (NGOs, faith-based organizations, community groups) and where relevant, private sector enterprises and associations. Good governance is firmly based on the principles of subsidiarity and engaging the right actors and stakeholders at the right 'level'. In many situations, establishing the practice of good governance entails setting up new procedures and institutions and changing (devolving) responsibility chains and reporting structures.

HABITAT AGENDA

The United Nations 'Summit on Human Settlements' in 1996 adopted the Habitat Agenda, a Global Plan of Action that focuses on ways and means of ensuring adequate shelter for all and managing sustainable human settlements in an urbanizing world.

HUMAN RESOURCE DEVELOPMENT

See *Capacity building*.

INFORMAL SECTOR

The informal sector of the economy embraces all the trade, commercial and manufacturing enterprises, including rental housing, that are not formally registered, regulated, licensed or taxed. These are usually small or medium sized, undercapitalized and operating at low levels of productivity though costs, including wage rates, are low compared to the formal sector. Health and safety conditions are usually precarious and there is generally no form of job security. These conditions give informal sector enterprises their competitive advantage over the formal sector, with which it often collaborates in the provision of down-stream goods and services. Insensitive attempts to support informal sector enterprises often lead to a degree of 'formalization' that increases costs and puts them out of business.

INNOVATION

Innovation is seen as a major influence on regional competitiveness within a knowledge economy. This is because innovations can create new products or services, or improve their quality or reduce the costs of production. Innovations can be technical or they can be administrative. **Administrative innovations** are about management and only relate indirectly to the basic work processes. An example might be the introduction of targets and performance measures. Innovations can be product innovations, namely, new products or services to meet the needs of customers or others outside the firm itself, or they can be process innovations. **Process innovations** are new ways of producing the product or delivering the service – for example, creating new structures to consult the public about local government policies. Thus innovation is not just a matter for business, but can also be a driver for the work of public sector and voluntary organizations. Innovations can be incremental (small changes) or radical (fundamental changes). Innovation is not a straight line process leading from an idea, through development to implementation. It is more likely to be the outcome of a lot of interactions (especially across professional or organizational boundaries), feedback and user involvement. It requires a willingness to experiment and to learn, including the confidence to learn from mistakes.

INSTITUTIONAL DEVELOPMENT

See *Capacity building*.

INTERREG

A European Union (EU) programme that provides matching finance (including staff time) for participating partners such as local authorities that are engaged in regional cooperation. **INTERREG III** runs from 2000–2006 and is designed to strengthen economic and social cohesion by fostering the balanced development of Europe through cross-border and inter-regional cooperation. INTERREG IIIA is about cross-border cooperation between adjoining regions. INTERREG IIIB supports transnational cooperation between national, regional and local authorities. INTERREG IIIC is concerned with inter-regional cooperation to improve effectiveness of regional development policies through large-scale information exchange and sharing of networks.

LEADERSHIP

Too often leadership is seen to be earned simply by age and status. Leadership in fact requires skills, which are not automatically bestowed by experience of doing a job. **Communication skills** are essential. Leaders need to be able to hold a vision of future possibilities and to present that vision in a way that others can understand and relate to. Leadership also involves valuing the rest of the team and making sure that everyone knows what is expected of them, what support and rewards they can expect and that their contri-bution is valued. Leaders must be able to inspire confidence and have credibility. They should be role models. They will also be figureheads and representatives, and must be aware of this at all times. Leadership also means taking responsibility, especially when unpopular decisions have to be taken.

LEARNING NETWORK

Networks are now recognized as being extremely important. The essence of a network is that the members can access the combined resources of the network, and that they do not necessarily need to be physically close together to do this. The advent of telecommuni-cations is one reason, but not the only reason, for the growth of networks. Learning networks therefore are means through which people learn together and are able to exchange experiences that are rich sources of knowledge and understanding. Through networks people can teach each other. Just as in a transport network, where interchange points that connect different networks together are the focus of intense activity, so in learning networks, connections into other related but different networks offer rich possibilities of opening up new insights and connections. There has been a paucity of learning networks in planning and urban development, and those that exist (such as professional bodies or campaigning NGOs) are not necessarily globally networked and interconnected. If skills are to be advanced and disseminated quickly, then international knowledge networks need to be consciously fostered and supported.

LIFELONG LEARNING

The world and the workplace change. Such changes mean that the knowledge and skills learned at the start of a career can become obsolete. Learning should be a process that continues throughout a career. It happens on the job as well as in the classroom. Lifelong learning is what is likely to make a good **reflective practitioner**, who is able to adapt to change and through self-awareness develop new knowledge and skills. For professionals, lifelong learning may be part of a requirement to undertake *continuing professional development* to maintain professional competence. This should involve identifying your own learning needs, planning how these can be met, then self-monitoring implementation. Non-professionals who have been active in civil society organizations and NGOs are likely to have acquired some lifelong learning through that experience. Systems that recognize the value of such experience are known as **accreditation of prior experiential learning**, and are important means to make professional qualifications accessible to a wider range of people than those who can afford conventional entry routes through full-time attendance in higher educational institutions. **Distance learning**, whether through studying printed or web-based materials, is another means of undertaking lifelong learning while continuing work in a job, NGO or as a carer, for example.

LIVELIHOODS

Livelihoods are all the assets and resources upon which households can draw in order to sustain their existence and development. Income and savings are important components, but so are such resources as access to social and welfare services, free schooling and health care, all of which contribute to *poverty alleviation*. Another fundamental contributor to livelihoods is **social capital**, which describes the strength of informal and semi-formal social networks such as extended families, close-knit tribal and ethnic support groups, membership of faith-based allegiances and neighbourly ties that can provide **social safety nets** in times of individual or community crisis.

MANAGEMENT SKILLS

Management skills are the skills involved in managing resources. This means managing time (for example, ensuring deadlines are met, that there is enough time to do the job and so on); finances (for example, budgeting so that money is used efficiently and that value for money is achieved); and people (which includes motivation, training and ensuring optimal performance of essential tasks). These skills are not just the responsibility of senior officers in an organisation; everybody is a manager and the skills involved in management are *generic*.

MAINSTREAMING

Often innovations or new concerns can be developed through short-term pilot projects or are seen as the responsibility of one particular part of an organization; for example, equality of opportunity can be seen as a matter for an 'equalities unit' within a local authority. In contrast, mainstreaming involves 'embedding' such concerns and practices so that they become integral to the outlook and routines of everybody within the organization. They are normal practice. To achieve this requires unambiguous endorsement from senior managers, clear statements of policy, a willingness to provide training so that everybody understands the innovations, why they are important and how they impact on their own work. As with any step change, there should be monitoring to establish how well the new concerns have been translated into mainstream practices. See also 'Gender needs and roles'.

MEDIATION

Mediation is a means of resolving disputes. It is often seen as an alternative to using costly legal processes to settle conflicts. In mediation a neutral person or agency helps the different parties to reach a negotiated settlement. The mediator should be acceptable to all the parties to the dispute, and will need skills. These include organizational skills, such as ensuring that the process of mediation is kept on track, and creating an environment for discussions in which the parties to the dispute feel comfortable. There are also cognitive and analytical skills, such as understanding agendas and hidden agendas, and the ability to synthesize complex information and make it easily understandable. Last but not least, interpersonal skills are required. These include the ability of deal with difficult situations and people, to 'think on your feet' and deal with the unexpected and to inspire confidence in the process.

MILLENNIUM DEVELOPMENT GOALS

The MDGs were the principal outcome of the United Nations Millennium Declaration endorsed by 147 heads of states and governments in September 2000. There are eight goals: 1) Eradicate extreme poverty and hunger; 2) Achieve universal primary education; 3) Promote gender equality and empower women; 4) Reduce child mortality; 5) Improve maternal health; 6) Combat HIV/AIDS, malaria and other diseases; 7) Ensure environmental sustainability; and 8) Develop a Global Partnership for Development. Each has a series of quantifiable targets and indicators. Virtually all the 18 targets have a bearing on the planning and management of human settlements, though of most direct significance are targets 10 and 11 to 'reduce by half the proportion of people without sustainable access to safe drinking water' and to 'achieve significant improvement in lives of at least 100 million slum dwellers, by 2020', both of which support Goal 7 that deals with environmental sustainability.

MONITORING

Monitoring is the process of regularly collecting, analyzing and evaluating information to measure performance, progress or change. Monitoring requires the selection of appropriate indicators, that is, measures that reasonably reflect the desired outcome, are reliable and can be understood, and that can be collected easily. Selection and interpretation of indicators is crucial, especially for monitoring organizational performance, since practices are likely to be shaped to produce a good score on the performance indicator, which may not be the same as delivering a good service.

NEGOTIATION

Negotiation is a process of reaching consensus by exchanging information, bargaining and compromise. Negotiation can happen when two or more parties have some shared interests but also some conflicting interests: if there are no shared interests then compromise is unlikely to be achieved. Negotiation may involve a neutral person or agency acting as a facilitator, as in the example of *mediation*, but it also occurs without the assistance of such help. Negotiation skills are likely to include a capacity to understand the issues that divide and unite the parties, to scope the range of acceptable solutions, to communicate effectively, and a willingness to compromise.

ORGANIZATIONAL DEVELOPMENT

See *Capacity building*.

PARTICIPATION and PARTNERSHIPS

Participation is the involvement of people in the planning and management of development programmes and projects. There is a wide range of levels of participation, extending from perfunctory consultation or 'using' people as unpaid labour to deliver projects cheaply (participation as a means) to engaging people, community leaders and their organizations in the design and management of development initiatives to the extent that they take a measure of control over the process (participation as an end). Even in this situation, however, the 'participants' are participating in someone else's (government's) initiative.

Partnership, on the other hand, implies shared responsibility, shared risks and shared benefits – partners have equal status, though they may, and usually do, have different roles and interests. In these circumstances government and communities are in it together, they both 'call the shots' on an equal basis. However, 'partnership' has taken pride of place in the current development jargon and is wildly and indiscriminately used to cover everything from subcontracting to the most outlandish excesses of political arm-twisting.

PLANNING AID

Planning aid is a system of voluntary provision by planners of free professional advice or training to individuals or groups that are unable to afford to pay for the full costs of such advice. Planning aid can be a means of developing understanding and skills and so contribute to enabling and empowerment. To be effective Planning aid also needs organizational skills and support – for example, to publicize the service, to put clients in contact with volunteers with appropriate knowledge and skills, and to evaluate the impacts of the service, including monitoring who are the beneficiaries.

POVERTY

Absolute poverty is the condition in which individuals and households have insufficient financial and subsistence resources to fulfil their basic need, such as the World Bank's crude but effective benchmark of a-dollar-a-day and definitions based on minimum consumption of calories.

Relative poverty is more complex as it allows for minimum needs to be revised as standards of living in society alter and acknowledges that the perception of poverty depends upon culturally determined criteria. The extent of poverty is not just a low level of monetary resources. Vulnerability, marginalization, the absence of social safety nets and social capital all contribute to poverty and the inability of the chronic poor to climb out of poverty. Similarly, the lack of access to urban services (education, health and welfare facilities) and exposure to environmental and social degradation (endemic disease, crime, violence) sustain and deepen urban poverty.

Poverty alleviation programmes set out to address the severity of these social impacts of poverty but do not necessarily attack the root causes of poverty.

Poverty reduction or eradication strategies, on the other hand, are to do with generating incomes and creating wealth (monetary and social) that enables the urban poor and their children to leave poverty behind them. Effective and sustainable poverty reduction is inextricably tied to urban economic growth and development.

POVERTY REDUCTION STRATEGY PAPERS

PRSPs have been promoted and supported by the World Bank and International Monetary Fund (IMF) in the 60 countries classified as 'highly indebted and poor' (HIPC) as the basis for concessional assistance. They lay out the country's macroeconomic, structural and social policies and programmes to promote growth and reduce poverty, as well as associated external financing needs. PRSPs are prepared by governments through a participatory process involving civil society and their principal international development partners. Because the populations of the majority of HIPCs are still rural, the PRSPs tend to concentrate on rural and regional strategies for poverty reduction at the macro level, ignoring the current trends in the urbanization of poverty. They sidestep the differences between the urban poor, where the poor live in cash economies with only marginal non-monetary supports, and the rural poor, the majority of whom have access to the basic products of subsistence agriculture and traditional social networks and supports.

PROCESS RE-ENGINEERING

Changing the way that things are done and routine procedures operate, requires a focused and planned approach based on analysis, experiment and monitoring. **A process map** needs to be prepared that shows the main steps in the process (for example, handling a planning application) and the various subprocesses. Such maps should help to identify the bottlenecks and problems in the process and prompt ideas about causes and remedies. In view of the need to enhance skills and capacity, the process mapping can be done to identify what skills are required at each stage, at what level the skill is needed and to audit the existing skills available to do the task. Process re-engineering can be used in this way to plan training and human resource development.

REGENERATION

Regeneration means halting and reversing the decline of urban or rural areas that is caused by a process of private and public disinvestment in them. Regeneration is about restoring the confidence of residents, property owners, businesses and investors in the area's future. Urban regeneration thus requires skills in understanding property markets and market signals, and of building visions and implementing actions that can bring about lasting improvements in the economic, social, physical and environmental conditions. Successful regeneration typically involves integrated actions, for example, embracing *social inclusion* not just property development.

SECURITY OF TENURE

Security of tenure to land and property is absolutely essential to the sustainability of any urban development process. If a household or enterprise has any doubt concerning its right to occupy and use of the land on which it is located or of property in which it is housed, they will neither care for it nor invest in it, or the neighbourhood in which it is located. Security of tenure does not necessarily mean outright individual freehold ownership of land. There are many forms of collective or cooperative ownership and leasehold titles that are secure and socially acceptable guarantees against forced eviction. Formal title deeds are not the only form of security that can stimulate the development of settlements by the households and communities that occupy them. The mere force of numbers in large squatter settlements can ensure that they cannot be evicted. In many cities formal and informal housing and land markets operate side by side. However, a legally recognized title deed does allow its holder to use his or her property as collateral for borrowing in formal capital markets and it generally increases the property's market value.

SITES AND SERVICES

Sites and services is an approach to making newly serviced land available for the construction of housing by low-income householders themselves. Based on the principle of *subsidiarity*, it recognizes that most individual households are unable to assemble land and access infrastructure and services, but they are able to procure their own houses. Thus government acquires land, subdivides it into plots and provides basic infrastructure (water, sewerage and so on) and services (schools, clinics and so on). The beneficiary households are awarded plots on which they construct houses to meet their needs and to the standards that they can afford. The plot size and level of service provision varies widely depending on local standards and the affordability of beneficiaries. For instance, in order to make them affordable plot sizes in some Indian sites and service projects have been as small as 25 square metres. Initial service levels range from the provision of communal water points and toilets shared by as many as 50 households and little else, up to the construction of substantial fully serviced core houses onto which the beneficiaries build their own extensions.

SLUM UPGRADING

Upgrading involves the progressive improvement of the physical, social and economic environment of a settlement. It is for the benefit of existing residents, with minimal disturbance or displacement. It involves the adaptation of an existing layout to incorporate improved facilities and infrastructure and does not involve major redevelopment (or slum clearance). Improvement of infrastructure networks (water supply, drainage, sanitation, roads/footpaths, street lighting, refuse disposal and so on) is typically a major component of any slum upgrading project. However, the first principle of effective upgrading is that households must be given *security of tenure* to their land and property. Upgrading must be a *participatory* process in response to the demands of the community, its leaders and individual households in order to assure its sustainability. If it is not, infrastructure improvements will be under-used or vandaliszd, people will become disillusioned with local government, and investment in the upgrading process will be wasted. To ensure the sustainability of physical infrastructure (maintenance, management and continuous development), it is important that investment in civil works is complemented by community development programmes to help develop local social cohesion and organization, and local economic development.

SPATIAL PLANNING

Spatial planning is a term that has been used particularly in Europe to identify a form of planning that seeks to analyze and influence the distribution of activities in terms of their location. It is concerned with the connections between places. Spatial planning seeks to manipulate relationships between places and to coordinate activities between spatial scales so as to promote economic development but also **territorial cohesion** and *sustainable development*. Spatial planning operates on the presumption that conscious integration of (particularly public sector) investments in sectors such as transport, housing, water management and such like is likely to be more efficient and effective than uncoordinated programmes in these different sectors.

STAKEHOLDERS

Stakeholders are the persons and organizations who have an interest in a policy or area. They may be affected by the outcomes or they may have a part to play, in which case they are often referred to as 'actors'. *Governance* involves government bodies working with stakeholders and understanding their needs and aspirations. Working with stakeholders implies rather different skills and attitudes than working for clients. A client hires a professional because the professional has expert knowledge and skills to look after the client's interests. Working with stakeholders, however, involves recognition that stakeholders are likely to take an active role in decisions, and are the best judges of their own interests. Thus professionals working with stakeholders need to understand diversity and have skills in engagement, *negotiation* and *mediation*.

STEP CHANGE

A step change means change that is significant and entails new outlooks and approaches. It is not slow, incremental and evolutionary change that follows a steady trend; rather this is change that departs from past norms in important respects.

SUBSIDIARITY

Subsidiarity is the principle of recognizing and allocating responsibility to the 'lowest effective level' of decision making. The lowest effective level is the level that engages the greatest number of users or beneficiaries in the decisions that are made. Decisions that are made at too high a level or too low a level are unlikely to be effective or the results to be efficient. For instance, decisions about a dwelling can only effectively be made at the level of the household; those concerning a neighbourhood, such as the use and location of public open space, at the level of the community; those to do with water or power distribution networks at the level of the municipality; and those to do with trunk infrastructure can only be effectively and efficiently determined at the regional or national level. The principle of subsidiarity underpins all aspects of good governance.

SUSTAINABLE DEVELOPMENT

There are five aspect of sustainability that impinge on the development of settlements, towns and cities. All should be taken into account in assessing the sustainability of any development.*

*From: Allen, A. & You, N., *Sustainable Urbanisation: Building the Green and Brown Agendas*, DPU, London, 2002, Box 1.2, p.6

Economic sustainability relates to the capacity to put local/regional resources to productive use for the long-term benefit of the community without damaging or depleting the natural resource base on which it depends and without increasing the city's ecological footprint. This implies taking into consideration the full impact of production cycles.

Social sustainability refers to the fairness, inclusiveness and cultural adequacy of an intervention to promote equitable rights over the natural, physical and economic capital that support the livelihoods of communities, with particular emphasis on the poor and traditionally marginalized groups. Cultural adequacy means the extent to which a practice respects cultural heritage and cultural diversity.

Ecological sustainability pertains to the impact of urban production and consumption on the integrity and health of the city-region and global carrying capacity. This demands long-term consideration between the state, dynamics of environmental resources and services, and the demands exerted over them.

Physical sustainability concerns the capacity of an intervention to enhance the liveability of buildings and urban infrastructures for all city dwellers, without damaging or disrupting the urban region environment. It also includes a concern for the efficiency of the built environment in supporting the local economy.

Political sustainability is concerned with the quality of governance systems guiding the relationship and actions of different actors among the previous four dimensions. It implies the democratization and participation of local civil society in all areas of decision making.

TERRITORIAL COHESION

Territorial cohesion aims to promote balanced development across a territory – that is, a political unit. The territory could be transnational, like the European Union, national or regional. Territorial cohesion means that citizens can have broadly similar access to important economic and public services regardless of where they live and work. Increasing regional competitiveness, inter-regional cooperation and better integration of policy for different sectors and across different scales of government (for example, through *spatial planning*) are seen as ways to promote territorial cohesion. Skills in **territorial impact assessment** are used to identify what impacts a policy will have on different territories – for example, linking capital cities by fast trains increases **territorial cohesion** at transnational scale but decreases territorial cohesion within a country unless the quality of secondary transport networks can also be upgraded. Territorial cooperation through programmes like *INTERREG* enables local and regional authorities to work together on shared concerns across national borders, to increase territorial cohesion.